OBEYVILLE SNOOP

Obeyville Snoop

Julia Ray

2bcreative

Obeyville Snoop

First Edition
Copyright © Julia Ray 2021

All rights reserved. No part of this publication may be reproduced, stored in a retrieval system, or transmitted, in
any form, or by any means, electronic, mechanical, photocopying, recording, or otherwise, without the prior
consent of the publisher.
Sale of this book without a front cover may be unauthorized. If the book is coverless, it may have been reported to the publisher as "unsold or destroyed" and neither the author nor the publisher may have received payment for it.

http://www.fastpencil.com
Printed in the United States of America

First Printing, 2021

CONTENTS

- One 1
- Two 6
- Three 11
- Four 16
- Five 21
- Six 28
- Seven 31
- Eight 34
- Nine 40
- Ten 43
- Eleven 49
- Twelve 54
- Thirteen 57
- Fourteen 60
- Fifteen 65
- Sixteen 69
- Seventeen 74
- Eighteen 81

- Nineteen 90
- Twenty 94
- Twenty One 101

ONE

If I had known this week would end up the way it did, I would have hand cuffed myself to my chair at home. Then none of the circumstances could have happened that cost me my best friend. Curiosity got the best of me. I must get her back.

I like to walk along the Sappa Creek, a beautiful creek that meanders through the south side of Obeyville, Kansas. Though these days not a whole lot of water fills the creek banks. It gets less and less every year. We need a few good steady rain seasons. Our farm fields need moisture. In this farm community, if they don't have a good crop season than they don't buy art, knick knacks, and books in my family store.

The winter brought little snow fall as well. It was like having Spring and now Spring is Summer. I believe Mother Nature is confused.

The kids don't know what it is like to have a foot of snow. They think an inch is exciting. I haven't had to buy snow boots in the last two years. I can't say I miss the blistering cold temperatures but a good snowfall would be great. I miss sledding.

My friends and I would slide down the steep creek bank which zoomed us across the frozen water to the other side. We would giggle all the way and hope the ice wouldn't break. It wasn't but a foot deep but it would freeze one's buns.

I like to explore, it makes me feel like I am ten again with no concerns. I suppose you would think a twenty-five-year-old woman would rather be chasing men and hanging out in bars, not me. I would rather be outdoors and learning. I'm like a sponge, soak in every bit of information I can. I have an entire room in my house devoted to books. I call it the Library Cave, some people have Man Caves, I have a Library Cave.

Yes, I am a nerd. A reborn nerd. I did my share of partying and being on the wild side in my High School days. I want to be nerd now, more relaxing and better for your health.

My work day is spent inside catering to customers at least five days a week, sometimes more. My parents own the store but I manage it so they can live their golden years fishing or whatever they want. I'm a good child like that. Nah, I just didn't want to go to college, yet. I know someday I will just have no desire right now.

I love my customers, but occasionally I get that one bad apple to ruin my day. I then head to the creek, stand in the middle of the thick lush trees, and yell at the top of my lungs to get my frustration out. The fresh air and exercise are an added blessing. A wonderful stress reliever. I sometimes bring a book with me and sit in one of the many trees along the creek and get lost in the story. I imagine I am the main character and it becomes one adventure after another. If only life was that way.

Today I walked to the edge of the bridge and made a sharp right turn where a well-traveled grassy path led into the dense trees. It's a wonder that I like to come down here because I really am extremely afraid of snakes. Luckily, I have not come across one, alive or dead. As I walked along the path I had to keep shoving the branches out of the way. They are getting overgrown, mental note to trim them back next time. Don't want my path blocked.

A shiver ran down my spine from the chill of the shade trees. I wish I had brought a jacket. When I stepped out my front door after work, the sun was warm on my face. It didn't occur to me that the thick of the trees would be a different story.

The branches snapped loudly under my tennis shoes. The previous adventure the sticks kept poking in through the sandal holes. Glad I didn't wear those again.

On the right side of the path is the old crooked tree that we would play truth, dare, or double dare when we were in grade school, it was coined the Love Tree, hence all the initials carved in it. I touched the initials that I carved into the tree of my first crush. Ah, the memories.

At the base of the tree a bunch of sting weed surrounds it. A person gets their skin next to that and it is like itchy non-stop for a few days. I laid in some without thinking once, never again. Itched in places no person should have to scratch.

A twig snapped behind me. I twirled around.

"Who's there?" I asked.

No answer, and I couldn't see a thing. Instant panic. I could run down the path I was going down, but then I will go deeper into the woods and may not find a way out. Whoever it is, came down the path I had. I looked around for a big tree branch to defend myself. Crap, all baby twigs.

Maybe I should drop to the ground and get as low as possible, maybe then he won't see me. Sting weed, I don't want to go there again. It made me itch just thinking about it. I'll hide in the shadows of the trees.

Another twig snapped.

I could see a shadow of one person. He was tall, masculine built, wearing a hat and far enough away I couldn't make out the face. He slowed his pace down. I moved behind a tree. I hope he didn't see me or is far enough behind me that he may not even know that I am here.

Duh, I spoke, so he must know the general direction. Idiot I am, number one rule don't ask the hunter if they are there. Looking behind me I saw a fallen tree along the ground. I will crawl across. It leads to the other side of the creek. Then work my way around him and get back to the path and run like crazy back to my house. My house is only a block away, an easy run. I can get help then.

I ran for the log. Oh, please let me get out of here. I didn't hear him moving anymore. The log was big enough for both feet side by side. Thank goodness it is only a foot above the water or I would say the heck with it and take my chances with the mystery man. Objects in the air with narrow walking space is so not my thing.

I wobbled a bit making my heart race. I kept thinking about him being right behind me and grabbing me. I got to the end, stepped off the log and turned around to see if I could see him. If I can't see him then maybe he can't see me. The early Spring leaves on the trees created a maze of hiding places. I couldn't see anything and could only hear the breeze on the tree tops.

I ran along the creek a good few minutes and then jumped across a narrow passage of water to get back to my side of the creek. I didn't bother to look back. I had one goal in mind and that was to get back to the path. I ran through the tall weeds praying for no snakes. I heard feet hitting the ground behind me. My heart pounding and my mind telling me to run faster. I felt a hand grab my arm, I swung around, losing my footing and falling to the ground. My head smacked the ground with a thump, and then the world went dark.

TWO

Oh, what a splitting headache!

I sat up slowly rubbing the back of my head trying to make it feel better. It wasn't working, felt like a bad hangover. I looked around but I couldn't see much in the small, dark room. Where the heck am I and who the heck hit me? Wait, I fell, but someone had grabbed me.

I hate dark places. I shivered thinking about what could be lurking in the corner. Like a dummy, I didn't tell anyone what I was doing tonight. It is only Friday so no one will miss me until Monday morning when I should be opening the store. Mental note, make sure to leave a note on my kitchen table to where I venture off to next time.

I moved to my hands and knees and began to move along the floor. A foul smell was coming from my left side. Moving my hand around I touched something cold and smooth. I felt a latch. Leaning next to it to make sure no animal noises were inside. It would be the pits to have an animal jump out. No noise. I unhooked the latch slowly opening the lid.

That's worse than spoiled food!

I slammed the lid back down. Covered my nose and did my best to not be sick. A lovely symptom to add to my splitting headache, a true hangover without the fun beforehand. After the smell faded, I began crawling again. Felt a slight breeze on my face, maybe I am close to the doorway. Bumped into something in front of me. Decided to stand up feeling all the way up. Moved my hand to the right, a door knob.

Relief.

I turned it, unlocked. Opened the door slowly, trying to not make a creaky noise. Light and freedom, almost.

"I was hoping you would be waking up soon. I have supper all ready for us." said the stranger, "Come join, before it is cold."

He was tall, blue eyes, and dark brown hair. The most amazing eyes, I might add. The bluest of blue. Reminded me of the clearest ocean waters. I couldn't stop staring at them.

"Why was I shut up in there?" I asked staring at him.

He looked at me and smiled.

"It was not locked, was it?"

"Well, no. That isn't the point." I said getting irritated, "I remember falling down. Why I am here?"

He stood up from the table and began walking towards me. I stepped back reaching for the door knob behind me. I was thinking that I could at least put the door between me and him. He stopped, seeing that I was going to turn into the room I had come out of. He stared at me. I stared back. It seemed like an eternity went by. He let out the most annoying laugh, turned around, and sat back down at the table. I don't like playing games. He is irritating the heck out of me despite his gorgeous looks.

"Well, I am famished. Stand there all night if you like, the food will get cold." he said.

Night? So only a few hours have went by? Or has days gone by? Is anyone out looking for me? The biggest question, are we in Obeyville?

The food smells amazing and is making my tummy grumble. I do need energy if I am going to get out of here. It would be smart to eat. I suppose if he poisons me, I will at least enjoy the food.

I cannot figure out why he is acting as though I am not a prisoner.

"If you sit down and eat, I will answer what is obviously asking in your pretty little head." he said looking at me.

"I am only eating because skipping meals is not good." I said as I plopped down in the chair across from him. He grinned still looking at me while placing the baked chicken on the steamy white rice on his plate.

I reached for the bowl of rice and put two big helpings on my plate, yes I like rice. Added the chicken on top just like his. The whole time he watched me. I hate that. I dove in savoring every bit of the meal. Oh, he can cook. The chicken had so much flavor and so moist. I closed my eyes and heard him chuckle.

"That good, huh?"

I glared at him.

"Just hungry. Don't flatter yourself."

Arrogant and good looking.

While enjoying the meal, I scanned the small cottage. There were a lot of photos of nature and no portrait ones. One photo had the most brilliant purple stone on a beach setting. It was dazzling.

The place had small windows with lacy curtains, not typical of a man's bachelor pad. Great, he is probably married and she is going to come through that door thinking we are having an affair. I glanced at this left hand, no ring and no tan line. Possibly, not married or doesn't like jewelry. I know a few that do not wear their rings.

"No, I am not married." He flashed his left hand at me. I believe my mouth dropped a few feet.

I looked away feeling embarrassed. I scanned the room some more. Next to my so called dungeon, looks to be a bedroom. This room is an open kitchen and living room design. In the front of the cottage by the front door is a bathroom. I could probably fit this entire house into my living and kitchen areas of my house. I feel trapped because I have no flipping clue where I am at. Woods? Another planet perhaps?

Through the windows the sun was going down. I could try to escape when it gets dark. Though I would not be able to see much of my surroundings, especially if we are out in the wooded area still. If I could get to the creek, I could try following it. It does run along the town edge.

Oh were has he taken me? Hate being out of control. Did he follow me from my house?

"Do you know who I am?" I asked. I might as well be blunt and to the point. He may answer and he may not.

He laughed that arrogant laugh.

"You said you would answer my questions."

Grinning, he reached for more rice. I grabbed the rice and set it down by my plate. He glared at me. It got his attention.

"Listen, I don't like games. I want some answers." I said angrily.

He stood up grabbing his plate and took it to the sink. I could see him scraping it off. Nice butt.

He set the plate down and turned towards me.

"You really do not remember me." he spoke irritated.

THREE

Normally, I'm good with faces, so I can't believe I don't remember him that is if he is speaking the truth. It could be a way to toy with me.

"I don't remember you."

"I worked for a local farmer in the summer of 1999, you came out to the farm with a girl, she had blonde hair and blue eyes. Can't remember her name but I didn't forget you. We hung out on the farm and then went to a party that night."

"Hmm, the friend has to be Dorie but I'm not remembering the farm or party."

He looked at me with the most amazing grin on his face. My heart did a flip flop like I have never felt before. Why did that just happen? What is it about those blue eyes that make me weak in the knees?

Mystery man walked over to me. He leaned on the table inches from my face. I could feel the warmth of his breathe on me and smell the sweetest cologne. This man should make my blood boil with rage not set it on fire with lust. What the heck is wrong with me? He snatched me.

I stood up and stepped back. My heart racing and my hands shaking.

"I do not remember you, I'm sorry. I just want to leave." I spoke.

"I don't know if leaving would be too wise. See, when I found you a man had been chasing you and when I went out earlier he was still out there only with several others. I am not the guilty one. I put you in that storage closet in case he happened to come to the door asking questions. You were hidden in there if he would happen to come to the door."

I don't know if he is telling the truth. I was knocked out. I suppose in a way it would make sense. Explains not being tied up and that he allowed me to come out and eat. No guns laying around. Now what do I say or do.
    "Well, then I thank you for not leaving me there for him. Remember falling and my head hurting. Sorry. But how did you get me away from him if he hit me?"

A loud bang came from outside that made us both jump.

He ran over, grabbed my arm and led me back to the storage room. He shut the door behind us. Motioned for me to be quiet. He locked the door gently and put his arm on mine as if to tell me to stay still.

A knocking came from the front door. The door knob began turning. Several footsteps echoed on the hardwood floor. No one spoke. It's like they knew we would be hiding.

I could feel a sneeze coming. Crap. Doing everything I could to hold it in. I sneezed my funny half sneeze. Mystery man covered my face up in case there was another one coming. I normally do sneeze more than once, luckily this time I did not. Did he remember that from years ago? Why can't I remember?

A pair of footsteps came to the storage door and tried the knob. When it wouldn't turn, the person tried shoving on the door but luckily it didn't budge.

Mystery man motioned for me to follow him on hands and knees to the back of the room. He opened that metal box that smelled awful.

He motioned for me to crawl into the box. I shook my head no, not in that smelly thing. He motioned again with a rather angry look and whispered get in. I peered over the side of it and saw the bottom had been opened and there was a ladder leading down below. Just like out of an adventure novel! I smiled. Did my best to not think of the smell.

I climbed in. Placed my foot on the ladder rungs one after the other praying that they were not old and rickety. I looked up to see him closing the lid after him and locking it from the inside. Then when he got past the bottom of the box he closed that as well and sealed it with an extra bar lock.

It was airy and pitch black. It smelled musty and I could hear running water. My feet touched ground. After he was down, he took my hand and he led us closer to the water sound.

I hope those guys above don't find the box. I wonder how this place got here. Many questions popping in my head. Exciting. Terrifying.

His hand feels warm and fits perfectly around mine. I don't want to let go.

He dropped my hand, bummer.

Mystery man lit a small candle and placed it on a wooden table against the wall. He started opening tubs searching for something. He found a flashlight and shone it in my eyes. Bright light.

"I was hoping it wasn't dead. We will head further down the tunnel just in case they find the passage way. I don't think they will but better to be safe than sorry." He said looking at me and then blowing the candle out.

"Why didn't you just lock me in the room and answer the door?" I asked, thinking why go to all this trouble.

"Several of them, one of me if things went wrong."

I didn't know what to say or think. I am floored. This is like out of a spy movie. I guess I got my adventure I was wanting.

I shook my head in agreement and began to follow him down the cold, dark cave like tunnel. Just where it leads and what the story is behind this, I can't wait to find out. My heart won't stop racing from the unknown and Mr. Blue eyes.

FOUR

The flashlight shown a good distance in front of us. I could see a tunnel that stretched quite a ways and was round enough to possibly fit a dump truck through. The walls were pretty smooth like it might have been dug by man and not by nature.

"Did you know caves were one of the first shelters humans used? They were sometimes used for hiding and other times burials. I hope we don't come across a burial. It is thought most of the caves in existence today were created after the big Flood the Bible talks about." I rambled on not paying attention that mystery man had stopped and turned to look at me. I bumped right into him.

"You are just as talkative as you were back then. Let me guess, you are a book nerd." He said smirking.

I didn't like his tone.

"And what is wrong with that? I love knowledge. Knowledge is good. Caves happen to be rather interesting to me. I wouldn't have the courage to explore an unknown cave but one that has already been is great. My goal is to explore a cave in each state. Bucket list you know." I replied irritably crossing my arms over my chest.

"What happens if a state doesn't have a cave?"

He was enjoying this way too much. He is getting on my nerves, pretty blue eyes or not.

"I bet there is. I have to research it all yet. Have you never been in a cave until now?"

"No, I was busy helping my family farm when I was growing up. No time for playing and exploring. It was called work then play if there was time." He turned and started walking down the tunnel again.

What a snoot! No wonder I don't remember him, no fun.

"How far does this go?" I asked walking a few feet behind him.

"I'm not real sure. I only began exploring it recently. I bought the cottage a month ago. I discovered the entrance when I tried to move the box and found it was bolted down. I removed the bolts and was surprised when the box came up without the bottom. I then had to pry the bottom part up, it was stuck by heavier bolts. I was shocked to see the tunnel and that first room. I decided to keep the box there until I could find out information on it. After all, someone went through a lot of trouble to hide that passage way. Who would have thought a box was hiding a secret place?" He chuckled, "Do you know any stories from the local people that were perhaps passed down generation to generation?"

I began searching my memory of the stories my grandparents told me growing up. I loved hearing about times when family was the root of survival, not like today's world with big corporations. Our family goes way back to the beginning. Obeyville was begun in 1872, when my great, great, great grandpa came here and opened his mercantile store. The first in the area and still standing to this day. It is where I currently work as the manager. A lot of history in that building. The family has done a great job of preserving its history also. Love searching for new items to put for sale in the store. I even make a few and they have gone over good in the tiny town. Of course with the internet that helps to sell more items and not just rely on the small number of people, which seems to dwindle every year. Maybe this will put it back on the map, a great tourist gimmick. I have all kinds of ideas in my head for this.

"My grandpa once said there were tunnels built under part of the town but thought they had all been caved in. He usually joked about it so not sure he believed the tales. He said he didn't ever see any so till he saw evidence it was just a fun tale to pass along. He will be surprised when I tell him they do exist. I wish I had my camera for proof though."

"Well, when we get out of here alive, you can bring him back and show him. I wonder if my cottage has the only opening. Did he ever mention how long the tunnels were or how many openings?" Mystery man stopped to look at me.

"No, he didn't completely believe them so he didn't elaborate on it. It would be cool if we found some artifacts like tools or pottery. I could display them in my store. Just no tools made of human bones." I got the goose bumps just thinking of it.

"I think the museum would latch on to those first. Let me guess, you are also an art fanatic?"

I scowled at him. I think he enjoys making fun of me.

"What do you think the tunnels were used for?" I asked avoiding to answer his question.

"I have no idea. I was hoping to go through all those old trunks back there in search of some answers but had not had the time to do so. I guess we will learn as we go."

A weird sound came from behind me. I turned as he turned the flashlight behind us. A small creature was running to get out of the tunnel.

"A cave salamander." I said with great enthusiasm.

"You're not afraid of the creature?"

"Heck no. I use to have a mudpuppy who is a close relative of the cave salamander. Cute little things. Plus, we are in their environment and are intruding. Now, if we come across a snake or scorpion I will scream and run like crazy. Nasty things in my book."

"You are a different breed."

"What is that supposed to mean?"

"When you answer my previous question, I will answer yours?" he began to walk ahead laughing.

"Fine. Yes I love art. So what." I slapped my hands on my sides.

"I have never met a woman that loved the artsy stuff and could also handle shall we say, tom boyish stuff. Usually, the woman is prissy and afraid to get dirty and definitely not a salamander type person. She is usually more feminine. You are therefore a different breed."

"I had two older brothers that loved to treat me like on of them. They were always picking on me. I sometimes wondered if they forgot I was a girl. Most of my girlfriends lived out on farms until we were in Jr. High, so I had to play with the boys in the neighborhood. My grandmother was always complaining saying it didn't look proper for me to hang with the boys, but there wasn't anyone else. I would even save up my allowance to go buy Hot Wheels cars."

"Seriously? No Barbie dolls?" He chuckled.

"I did have Barbie dolls, just enjoyed the cars also. Like you said, I am a different breed."

He began walking again through the chilly long tunnel chuckling and shaking his head. I am so glad I can entertain him. NOT. It is going to be a long journey.

"Oh, my, look at that. I have never seen a more beautiful sight." Mystery man exclaimed.

I peeked around him to see what he was looking at. Wow, just like in the photography books.

FIVE

In front of us was the most amazing clear blue pond. A twenty foot waterfall cascaded into the pond at the far side. At the top I could see a bit of sunshine, it was beaming through an opening creating a glow on the water. It was absolutely beautiful. A photographer's dream shot.

I could be lost here for a few weeks and not care about anything else.

Looking at the water made my mouth thirsty. I ran over to the edge of the pool and cupped my hand and filled it with water. Mystery man ran over to me and hit my hand before I reached my mouth.

"Why did you do that?" I asked angrily and so wanting a drink.

"You don't know what is in there."

"At this point, I could care less. I need water, we need water to survive."

I went ahead and took a drink. It was divine. The best tasting spring water I have tasted. It is even better than country water. I decided to play like I was choking and fell to the ground with my hands over my throat. He ran over and grabbed me. I started giggling. He dropped his hands and walked away cussing.

"Hey, have a sense of humor. It's good to laugh in situations like this." I said sitting up.

He wouldn't talk but glare at me. He sat down on a big boulder next to the pond. Great, there is nothing worse than a grumpy man. I don't like him, a man must have a sense of humor.

"So are you ever going to tell me your name at least?" I said trying to break the silence.

"Brad, since you can't seem to remember." He growled.

"Nice to have a name with the face. Sorry I don't remember you. I was a teenager with many dramas going on back then."

"I know too well." He replied, throwing a small pebble into the pond.

He wouldn't even look at me. This will not be a fun adventure at this rate.

"What is that supposed to mean?" I snapped back.

He made a snort and began walking around the pond looking around. I got up and began to follow him because I wanted answers and for him to look at me. He turned around and looked right into my eyes.

"I am glad I am so forgettable. We did go out on a date. You sure know how to knock a guy's self-esteem down."

He stormed passed me and walked to the other side of the pond.

I don't recall going out with him. How the heck would I forget that? How could I forget those blue eyes?

I wish I had my phone to call my best friend, Dorie, she was there. She is at college now. She was disappointed when I didn't follow her to college. It was always the plan to go together since we were in Jr. High. I am just so glad we stay in touch and still do things when she comes home to visit. I would love to talk to her now. I need her wisdom and memory since mine is failing me.

"When did you say this was?" I asked. He gave me that evil look. I do believe I have hurt his ego.

"It was July 1999. I came to help my father's longtime friend, Carl Wilson, on his farm. You came out one day with a friend, young blonde, your age, about your height."

"It sounds like my best friend, Dorie."

"Carl introduced us and then you girls went on a ride in the harvest truck with me. You said you had never rode in one before," he chuckled, " I didn't care if it was a lie. I thought you were pretty cute for a young girl. Pretty, long brown hair, blue grey eyes, and unforgettable legs." He said looking at my legs which are thankfully covered by pants.

At least I made an impression, made me feel good inside.

"How old are you?" I asked.

"I'm old enough."

I knew he would answer with a smart remark.

"Seriously, how old are you?"

"I am the young age of thirty-five. I am not old and I know you are twenty-five."

He remembers my age. I am really starting to feel bad for not even remotely remembering a little bit of him. I began to look him over and he saw.

"I had blonde hair back then from being outdoors all the time. I am now an accountant so no more outdoors more like hello cubicle. And thanks to contacts, I no longer wear glasses."

A light bulb went off in my head.

"OH. Wow. I um....do remember you. I am now genuinely embarrassed." I turned away from him. Oh crap. He was my rebound from Damian. I began to pace.

"Oh crap, oh crap." I kept repeating in a low voice.

He walked over and took me by the arm. He looked me in the eyes, only inches from my face.

"You don't have to be embarrassed. Crap happens. It was only two weeks' time, not a lifetime like your old lover boy." Brad said sounding a bit jealous. How strange after all these years.

I could smell his sweet cologne again. How I have missed the smell of a man. It's been way too long not being near a man. I wanted to drift off into one of my novels where the man sweeps the lady off her feet with romance. If only the real world was like that. I do believe the last time we saw each other it was anything but romance. I remember being at the lake and getting drunk and fumbling hands. The rest I don't recall. I think if it would have been hot romance I would remember. I think.

I am pretty sure he was a rebound from Damien and I feel even more ashamed. I should have given myself time to heal. Damien was the love of my life gone sour after two years of dating. It seemed like a lifetime to a teenage girl. We dated from eleventh grade through my graduation, and then I caught him with another girl. He broke my heart and it still hasn't healed in ten years.

"Yes, lover boy is history. In fact, he is happily married to the girl he cheated on me with. I rarely party anymore. I apologize for any stupid things I did or said back then, even though I'm not sure what I did. I am glad I gave up partying, might have had many more cloudy memories if I hadn't. So, why did you leave after only a few weeks?"

"The job was done. I had to head back to my hometown to help my dad on his farm. I was going to come back the following summer but I decided to enroll in college. I picked a career in accounting, worked for a big firm for the last five years. Carl called and mentioned he needed some more help and I though why not. I quit my boring job and headed on down here. I have been here about a month. I am going to open my accounting business and then help Carl in the evenings and weekends. He is getting to where he can't do all the work and has no other family to help."

He was looking at his hands and had a look like he was hiding something. He is still a mystery, but it is a start.

"I think we should look around. I am hoping there is another tunnel that will lead us out," he said taking charge looking up at the opening above the waterfall, "I don't think we can get up there to climb out."

I looked up and shook my head no. My mind was still trying to recall ten years ago and wondering what else he is not telling me.

"We could always turn around and go back to your cottage. I mean surely they have left by now. We haven't heard any noises behind us. I think we would with the tunnels echoing." I said.

It sure would be nice to find something to eat. My stomach is growling.

"I thought about that. I am hoping they think we left a long time ago before they got there and are looking in the woods. Maybe we should stay here tonight just to be on the safe side. If we find no other way out then we can turn around and head back. Plus, I am curious about this underground mystery. If I had known this pond was here, I would have been coming for swims regularly. It is paradise." he replied.

We started searching around for anything.

"Hey, come look over here, I found a trunk. It has a lock though." I said with excitement.

He came over and tried to pull open the lid hoping the lock was old enough it would break from the thrust. It didn't. We looked around for something to possibly hit the lock and break it. He picked up a good size rock and hit it. The lock broke open.

Brad lifted the lid and the contents were what we needed. A bunch of nothing. Great. My tummy let out a huge growl. We busted out laughing and sat down on the ground. I looked up at the opening and saw the evening stars. We need to find some candles to save on the flashlight.

"Let's keep looking." I said not wanting to give up hope.

We looked on the other side of the pond, behind a pile of rocks, a tunnel led to a small room. I would say about 12 feet by 12 feet. Along the walls were shelves of canned food and other supplies.

We smiled at each other. Yes food!

I walked over to one wall and grabbed some blankets. No pillows, but we can use a blanket for a pillow, plenty of those. Brad found a couple kerosene lamps, and thankfully some matches next to them. Everything was on the shelves and there were no batteries or flashlights. The supplies seem to be from decades ago and more the old camping way.

"I wonder why all this stuff is here?" I asked, more thinking out loud than really wanting an answer.

"Good question, another mystery. Look, cans of food," Brad said picking up one and inspecting it, "Do they really ever go bad? I mean peaches are peaches, right."

"I think peaches will be alright. I'm starving so at this moment I don't care if they are expired."

I watched as he poked the lid with a knife and worked an opening on the can like he had done this before. He handed me a can, I reached in with my fingers and put a peach slice in my mouth. It wasn't exactly tasty, but it solved the hunger pains.

I decided to lie down on the ground. I fell asleep instantly and began dreaming of grilled steak and a tall glass of Pepsi.

Boy, I miss my Pepsi.

SIX

I woke up to Brad snoring. I glanced at my watch which said after 8a.m. I bet if I am quiet I can take a dip in that gorgeous pond. I need to, my hair is having a wild episode this morning.

I walked to the opposite side from where we slept and stripped my clothes off. I slowly stepped into the low part of the pond and waded in as quiet as I could.

Oh, heaven.

The water felt luke warm and nice on the body. Looking down, I could see the bottom through the crystal clear water but not sure how deep. I dove down to touch the bottom. The bottom was smooth and a copper color. I headed back up and turned to swim back to where my clothes were.

"What the heck?" I yelled seeing Brad in the water a few feet away.

"You are not the only one that needed a relaxing swim. It would be a crime to leave without enjoying this beautiful pond." he grinned that gorgeous smile.

That means he is naked, don't look down, oh too late. Whoa...

If I can see him than he can see me. Oh crappola.

"Oh, get over the shyness. We are two adults and naked bodies are art. Isn't that what your artistic side would say? Plus, I know your curves already." he replied winking at me.

I believe I turned ten shade of red.

"My curves, about that, I do not remember anything about that moment in time."

His smile turned to a frown.

"In time you will remember. Trust me."

He swam closer to me. He reached out to touch my face. He gently moved the hair out of my eye that decided to fall down.

I cannot lose control, I will not lose control.

"You are beautiful. The shyness is intriguing to me. A definite change from years ago. I have thought about you over the years." he said with gentle soft voice.

"That was the best pickup line I have ever heard." I said trying to maintain my hormones.

Charming men are the devil. They are hard to resist. I swore the next time I was with a man it would be in a relationship. Dang temptation!

He chuckled, turned around, swam back to where his clothes were. I watched his toned body move through the water, nice eye candy.

He climbed out of the pond without any hesitation knowing I was watching his every move. Nice buns! I must turn around, I need to turn around. Ok, I am not going to turn around. I can look. I am old enough. I guess I have seen them before. Dang, why did I have to be so drunk back then. He is one that should be remembered. I am an idiot.

"I take it you are liking the view?" he asked bringing me out of my trance.

I smiled and didn't have a comeback. Utterly speechless.

He picked up my clothes taunting me to come get them. Now he is being a butt.

Decisions. My arms and legs are getting tired wading here. Oh, hell, I dove under the water and swam to the shoreline.

I walked toward him pretending I was not naked. Pretending he was blind. Anything to not turn red again. He wrapped a blanket around me to wipe the water off.

"We better start exploring other things so we may find a way out." he softly kissed my neck. I almost fainted. Not the neck, my complete weakness. I opened my eyes and he was walking towards the other side of the pond.

I'm a bit disappointed, the hormones are raging, but we cannot go there right now. I quickly dressed and followed him to the other side.

SEVEN

Brad was in the supply room we found the previous night. The old trunks had quite a few books and papers that looked decades old. I was trying to forget about the naked scene while it seemed to have escaped his mind. He acted like nothing had occurred. Men.

"What did you find?" I asked sitting down on a long wooden bench along the opposite side of the room from him.

"This looks to be someone's journal from long time ago. The ink is readable but the writing is hard for me to read." He said, handing me the journal, "maybe you can read it."

I opened the journal to the front page seeing the name Catarina Marie Denton. I do not remember any Denton's living in Obeyville. Perhaps they all moved away before my time. This will make great bedtime reading when I get back home. If I get back home, starting to wonder.

"We probably should head back to the cottage? I would think the guys gave up by now or they would have caught up with us." I closed the journal placing it by my side.

"Depends on why they are chasing you. It's possible they are waiting in the cottage. I would like to explore further. I would think there is another way out."

Brad pointed to the right in a dark corner where a doorway stood. It had the most beautiful engraved door I had ever seen. I ran my hand down the engravings to the bottom of the door which had words.

"The Beyond Lies Beyond." I said out loud wondering what does that mean. Talk about igniting the curiosity.

"Let's find out." Brad said turning to me with a mischievous grin on his face, "but first we need some of this canned food." He went back to the shelves and put food into an old carrying bag that was on the shelf.

"I do like adventures. I hope there is another way out though. It is Saturday and I need to be home tomorrow night for work on Monday."

I filled another carrying bag with supplies and food. We grabbed the kerosene lamps and lit them up. We need to save what was left of our flashlight batteries. There might be places where we can't have the lamps.

Brad turned the door knob but it would not budge.

"Maybe it is locked, look for a key on the shelves?" I asked beginning to look around. I really want to see what is behind that door. Dang words have me beyond curious. We tore the trunks apart looking.

"I found one!" Brad said holding the key.

Then we heard distant voices coming from where the first tunnel we came through. We looked at each other with shocked faces. Crap.

Brad put the key in the door. Please work I kept praying. My anxiety reached a whole new level.

The door opened.

We stepped into another long tunnel. The kerosene lamps lit up enough to see a good ways. We kept the key with us and locked the door from our side. Hopefully, it will stop them for awhile. We need distance between them and us.

On the walls of the tunnel there were candles. No time to light them all though. Plus, think we should keep our matches for our lamps. My heart was racing. It was getting chilly the further we walked in the tunnel.

I turned to see if they had made it through the door, no lights. Good sign. This tunnel seemed to go on forever. When I turned back around I did not know Brad had stopped and I bumped into him. He didn't bother to turn or say anything because of the amazing thing at the end of the tunnel.

The Beyond.

EIGHT

"Incredible! How is it possible?" I said when I saw what Brad had stopped to look at.

A small stone village the length of maybe a football field. The ceiling of the cave had a few openings that was allowing the sun to shine down on the buildings. I wonder where those are up above ground. I need to explore that when I get home. I am not sure what direction we are in relation to Obeyville. I lost track last night once we were in the pond area. I forgot to sit and retrace our steps to figure it out. I was a bit preoccupied this morning.

Brad set his bag on one of the stone tables at the entrance of the first building. He lit one of the kerosene lamps.

"We better save our flashlight for the way home. We will need some light inside I assume. This exceeds what my grandma told me." He mumbled at the end.

"What did you say?" I asked.

"I hope there are some treasures inside." He was not looking at me. I swore he said something about his grandma. I think he knows way more about this place than he lets on. But why keep it a secret from me.

"We can explore each building beginning here. There are ten total, five on each side. This is amazing. We may end up famous for this." Off he went.

"What about the guys behind us? Do you think the door will hold?" I asked.

"I think it will buy plenty of time."

The door opened with ease. No fighting this one. It smelled musty and old like no one has been here for decades. Liquor bottles lined up on shelves in front of a mirror on our right side. Lots of tables and chairs in the middle of the room. Another door at the far end of the bar with a small stage to the side.

I went behind the bar picking up bottles and sniffing them. Alcohol. What kind I am not sure, I was a beer drinker. The labels are worn out. I am not brave enough to try them. I would hate to get sick down here with no help.

"Recognize any of them?" Brad asked sitting down on one of the bar stools.

"No, I am not familiar with liquors. One is fruity smelling which could mean a Schnapps but did they have that way back when. The others are whiskeys I am assuming."

"Hand me the clear one." I did. He opened it and took a big drink.

I stared in disbelief. He better not die on me. He made an awful face but took another drink. He is complete nuts.

"Now that is strong stuff. Not sure what but hopefully I will not get sick." He laughed and kept laughing.

"You die on me, I am going to haunt you when I die from being stuck in this cave world."

He laughed again. I believe he is drunk.

"If only there were snacks. Chips or pretzels would be awesome." He looked under the counter stumbling every step he took.

"Please do not mention food. I am hungry and canned food is not sounding good."

My energy level is draining. Probably the lack of sugar. I need my Pepsi. Hopefully, I make it through all the buildings before needing a nap. I sound like my grandma. She loves her naps in the morning, afternoon, and evening. Maybe she needs to take up drinking Pepsi.

"Quit complaining. It is an adventure! Lots to explore. I wonder why this is here. Why would they live down here? So much to find out." He said slurring his words. He slapped me on the back and stumbled to the door at the back of the saloon.

"I do believe you are drunk."

He pushed the door open with a loud thud. I rushed to make sure he did not fall down. There were stairs leading up.

"Oh, we might need that lamp." He said turning around, almost falling into me.

He breathed on me. Dang, some strong stuff. I could get drunk off his breath. I grabbed the lamp off the bar.

"Let me go first. I will hold the lamp, do not need you falling with it. No fire trucks down here." I passed him on the stairs.

"I am not drunk. I just a little tipsy."

"I am the fairy godmother." I rolled my eyes.

He laughed or rather snorted. At least I am humoring him. I wonder if this is what I looked like when I was drunk. It is different being the sober one. His head will hurt tomorrow. I do not miss that part.

I heard a bang against the wall behind me. I turned to see Brad leaning against the wall smiling like the cat who ate the canary. I shook my head, stepped down to help him walk up the stairs.

"Why thank you pretty lady. You come here often?" He touched my face.

We made it to the top of the stairs after missing several steps on the way up. He is heavy. A wide open room full of beds and dressers. Thank goodness. I will put him to bed to sleep this off and take a nap myself. He was out as soon as he hit the bed.

I searched a few of the dressers but they were empty. I was hoping to find books or photos. No clues to why this place is here. No bathroom. I hope Brad does not get sick, long way to the outside. I fell on to the bed next to Brad. Comfy, beats the hard surface from last night.

I sensed someone, opened my eyes and saw a white figure standing by my bed. I tried to yell but nothing came out. It stared at me. Brad was snoring. It looked like it was studying me. I pinched my leg to see if I was dreaming. Ouch. I ran over to Brad shaking him to wake up. The figure disappeared.

"What the heck do you want? Quit that!" He growled at me.

"I saw something but it is gone now."

He put his hand on his head and made a painful face.

"Dang, why did you let me drink that stuff?"

"Do not blame me, you are old enough to make your own choices."

He sat up looking around the room.

"Do you believe in spirits? I mean an old place like this might have a few flying around." I said. I think I will stay close to him until we are out of here.

"I suppose they exist. Our spirit goes somewhere when we die why not flying around. Why?"

"Old place brings up questions like that. It is like a ghost town."

Maybe I did not see it. I could be hallucinating from lack of sugar. The pinch was real but I have seen things before after waking up and they disappear. This place is a bit freaky.

"How long was I asleep?" Brad asked.

"I do not know, I fell asleep and have not looked at my watch since we found this place. I was a bit distracted."

"Is this the only room up here?"

"Yes and the dressers are empty too. When they left they did not leave a thing behind. Wiped clean. Not even a spider."

"There are more buildings to look through. Let's go." He grabbed the lamp and I stayed right behind him. I kept looking behind me expecting the white ghost to show up. I will not sleep tonight or ever.

We were about to step outside when a loud bang sounded by the stage. We both jumped knocking into each other. Brad pulled me behind him to protect me. The lamp did not give off enough light to see the stage area. We slowly walked towards it.

"It was only a chair falling over. No big deal." Brad said relief in his voice.

"How did the chair fall? It does not just fall over."

"Maybe there was a breeze from us walking by." He shrugged his shoulders. I do not think he believed that.

I headed for the door. It was enough for me to leave this place. I went to the table and sat down. I grabbed my bag and took out the peaches and a canteen of water.

"Good idea. Refill before the next building. I need to re-hydrate after that drunk episode. Did I say anything during that time?"

I shook my head no. Funny he should ask that. I did forget to try after I saw the beds.

NINE

The second building looked like a grocery store. Coolers, checkout stand, and shelves of food. I lifted a box of crackers off the shelf and took a bite. It was alright not flavorful. At least it is not peaches. The coolers were empty which I was glad for because that would smell awful with no power.

"Are you thinking what I am thinking? Coolers need power to run." Brad said.

"Very true, but how? I did not see any power lines on our way through the tunnels."

"Maybe a generator somewhere. I do not know."

Brad opened the last cooler and slammed the door shut. He backed up bumping into a row of shelves with canned goods knocking them onto the floor. It startled me.

"What is wrong?"

"Um, there is a hand in a jar. In fact, several of them."

I did not believe him. I opened the cooler. I gasped.

"What the heck?" I wanted to throw up. I wanted to run back to the cottage. I hope the person who had that hand is not down here somewhere. And the person who did the cutting is not still here.

"Maybe they were doing experiments on loss limbs. You do have to keep them cold, I think. Let's move on." he walked to the cash register pushed a button and the drawer opened up. It was empty.

"Too bad there was not cash in there." I joked to lighten the mood.

He picked up a ledger from under the counter. It was black leather bound. He opened it and there was handwritten notes.

"What is it?" I asked getting closer.

"A store ledger. There are products wrote down with prices beside them. The old way of keeping books before computers."

"My mom still does that. I did convince her to buy a computer but she makes me still fill out the ledger. She says it is backup because those things break all the time and she is not learning to run one." I chuckled.

"I bet in time she will change her mind. We learned the ledger in college but the computer definitely cuts back on the work and time."

"I doubt it, she is stubborn."

"I see where you get it from then." He smiled.

"Laugh all you want."

"Hey look here. This has the name Edgar Neshec signed on Jan. 21, 1946."

I grabbed the book. It can not be. Grandpa said he did not know anything about the tunnels under the city. It means he knows why those hands are in the cooler. I can not believe it.

"He is on several of the pages with different years." Brad said.

I am depressed now.

"I hope there is an explanation but it does not look good. I will be talking to grandpa."

TEN

Heading into the sixth building on this side, I can't help but wonder why all the stores and how long did the people live down here? So far, a person could survive forever as long as one didn't miss the sun much. And flowers and green grass and space. After awhile I think I would feel like a sardine in a can. The small opening above the pond and here are not enough outside world for me.

"Now this is my type of store, men's toys!" Brad said checking out the many guns on the shelves.

He picked up a handgun, spun the empty barrel, and placed it in his pants. He grabbed a box of bullets and a long blade knife.

I hate guns. Don't mind others having them as long as they are trained.

Brad picked up a bag off the floor and stuffed it with several guns, bullets, and more knives.

"Do we really need all that?" I asked.

"Remember the bad guys following us, plus, no one is here to tell us no. You took a shirt."

I rolled my eyes and walked out the door.

I could feel a breeze blowing through the small opening above. Felt nice. It's been a day but I'm missing my outside world. The grass, trees, sun and intelligent people.

"Next." Brad said walking into the other building.

Curiosity always wins with me. I followed.

Lots of hardware! Rope, nails, kerosene lamps, shovels, you name it, it is on the shelves.

Yep, a community could survive here.

If we end up stuck here, we have plenty of lamps for light, thank goodness. This place is way too dark at night for me.

Brad was taking his time looking at everything.

"Come on, three more buildings to go. I'm tired. I'm hungry."

"And grumpy." He said following me out the door.

Building eight, was a magnificent large indoor hot springs! Goldmine!

Along the pool edge were comfy lounge chairs perfect for a nap. White robes hanging on hooks on the wall behind the chairs. Feels like a spa. I chose a lounge chair placed my stuff underneath. I stripped down to nothing.

"Whoa, teasing much?" Brad asked keeping his eyes on me.

"Nothing you have not seen." I slid into the water.

Heaven. I swam to the other side and sat on a ledge in the water.

Brad dropped his jeans and boxers. Then the shirt. He swam up to me.

"Did you enjoy the show?"

"It didn't do a thing for me." I looked away.

He grabbed my hands and gently pulled me to him. The water was not deep. We could both touch the bottom. I was on my tipy toes though. Short person problems.

He put his arm around my waist pulling me in so I could feel every bit of him next to my skin. I shouldn't be doing this. I need to swim away.

I want this.

His warm lips touched my neck. The feel of his breathe moving up towards my ear made my head dizzy. I closed my eyes and lost myself to his touch. He nibbled sending chills through my body. I felt his lips touch mine. I returned the kiss passionately forgetting any anger towards him. My hands roamed, his hands roamed.

And then the unthinkable.

"Why Brad, that was not in the deal? You cannot have the whole package." Said a familiar voice.

Brad swiftly turned around leaving me with a gaping mouth. Dang it. I'm going to kick whoever that is. I peered around him and that's when I saw Damian. Beyond shocked and pissed.

"Yes, Annie, it is I. I see you are making the most of your time with Brad." Damien grumbled looking really upset. I believe the jealous monster is showing.

"You know each other? What the hell!" I shoved Brad out of my way and swam back to where my clothes were. I didn't think twice climbing out naked. I was too damn mad and hurt. Confused. I grabbed a robe and threw it on. I gave an angry look at Brad who was still standing in the water looking like he lost his puppy.

"I thought you were going to stay behind us?" Brad asked.

"Change of plans." Damian motioned for the other two men to grab me.

I was too confused to resist. I felt betrayed. What the heck is going on here? How do they know each other? What did he mean stay behind us?

Brad climbed out of the water and put his clothes back on. Damian walked over to Brad within inches of his face.

"I told you to not put a hand on her." Damian showed more anger than I have ever seen from him.

"You are the married one, not me."

Brad walked towards me, lips parted to say something, but I slapped him. Tears filled my eyes.

"All a game? Why?" I stepped away from him. I didn't want to be near him.

Damian approached me before Brad could answer. He moved a stray piece of hair from my face. I shivered feeling his touch after all these years. He makes me sick.

"How does it feel to be used?" Damian asked.

"Feels like the many times you did to me."

"Me? I think you remember things wrong."

"Who married the person that you cheated on me with?"

"I guess the dates with my best friend has slipped your memory."

"No, I call it sweet revenge." I stormed away from him and plopped down on the lounge chair. The two big goons followed me. Brad laughed. Damian shot him a look of warning.

I see he still can't admit his wrong doing. I admit I probably shouldn't have went out with his best friend, but hey, he showed me the attention that Damian didn't at the time.

I was tired of being his thing whenever she didn't want him. I'm glad he married her because it woke my butt up.

"I think you need to think things over a bit." Damian nodded to the two goons. They grabbed my arms and lead me to a door at the back of the hot springs. The husky brown eyed guy opened the door and pushed me in. The door closed behind and I hear a lock sound. Great.

I sat down on the cot, the only thing in the cold room. Dark shadows on the other side of the room. Normally, I would be scared but I am too pissed at ding dong out there. Make that two ding dongs. Why did he have to be involved in this mess? I have enjoyed life without him. I rarely see him in town. I think he hibernates on his farm. What the heck do I have to do with all this? And Brad?

The door flew open and in came Brad. Wonderful. He looked sad. Good. Jerk.

"I'm sorry. I had no intention of kissing you but when you stripped down, rather difficult to resist."

"Gee thanks. What about you knowing my ex?" I stared at the ceiling. I don't want to look at him.

"I met him when I first moved here. Carl told him I bought that cottage, they have land next to one another. Old family friends. It was Damian that told me about the tunnel entrance under the box. And it was him in the woods that knocked you out. He says you have something he wants from down here but knows you wouldn't give it to him. He thought I could gain your trust and get it. I'm not sure why things changed. I don't know what is going on now. He has not told me yet what the thing is. I was suppose to get to know you this weekend and then next week he would tell me. He doesn't know we have met before. I never told him."

"Why didn't you tell him?"

"A gut feeling. Glad I listened to it." He smiled.

I laid down on the cot and turned to the wall. My head hurts. Nap time. Think time. Plan to get the hell out of here and away from both.

ELEVEN

I slept longer than a nap. Woke up facing Brad's cot, but it was empty. Looked around. Heard the shower turn on. A shower sounds wonderful. Thinking about the conversation last night, I don't know whether to trust him. Feels like something is missing from his story.

"Amazing shower! Like a waterfall." Brad said walking out with a towel wrapped around his hips. Water beading down his chest.

This is so not fair. I want to not want him. He has to stop with the nakedness.

"Your turn. I imagine Damian and his goons will be here soon."

"Right, I was hoping it was all a dream."

Grabbed my clothes and into the bathroom I went. He should have considered that option.

I need to get home so I can find some answers. I will start with my family, they are hiding something.

I was dressed and read in time for Damian to walk in. I wonder what the story is with the two goons. He acts like a mob boss having them around.

"Ready for some walking after a rested night of sleep?" Damian asked getting close to me again. I would love to kick him in the balls. I am still angry at him. I am going to find out what he is up to and ruin it. I can play this game only better.

"I hope that means walking home. My parents are expecting me." I said.

"No, we have a few more buildings to explore. Then we will head home. I am sure your parents have not missed you since you like to take off for the weekends."

How does he know I leave on the weekends. The jerk has been keeping tabs on me? My blood pressure just spiked.

"What do you want from me?"

"In due time, no hurry. Isn't this place exciting? I think the next building will excite you even more."

I did not answer. At this point, I want to leave and think it is a nightmare. He led us to the next building.

"This one is for you. I did not think you would want to leave without seeing it. I turned the power on so you can see it in all its beauty." Damian said.

A library.

The wood carvings of the shelves were absolutely exquisite! They stood around twelve feet tall. I always wanted one of those ladders that slide across the floor. My house has low ceilings so it would not look right for my library. It would take years to read all the books here. I hate when Damian surprises me with something good. Dang him.

"I will leave you to explore for awhile. Brad follow me." And they left me alone with all these wonderful books.

I ran my fingers along the spines of the books reading the titles. A section on farming techniques, intriguing for a place that has no soil and little sun. Books on electrical, wood working, and intricate carvings. I grabbed one on intricate carvings thumbing through the pages. Beautiful, they do not make things like this anymore. I placed it back on the shelf and took a book from the rock section. The section was loaded with books. I grabbed the title Underground Rocks.

The three foot section opened to a secret passageway!

"Whoa! I definitely need one of these in my library."

I stepped in feeling for a light switch. Nothing. I took the flashlight out of my backpack that I found at the hardware building. The tunnel was narrow not like the ones we had been through. I shut the door behind me just in case no one knows about this but me. My secret from them since they have many. It would be terrific if it did lead to outside. I bet they would freak not finding me, then to find me at home. If only.

My tummy grumbled. We forgot to eat this morning with Damian showing up early. I know I have some peaches but I think I will wait to see where this leads to.

The flashlight flickered. Please do not go out. I don't like total darkness.

I sleep with my radio on and the curtains open. Looking at the moon and stars is a relaxing way to fall a sleep. The neighbors are far enough away they can not see in.

There went the flashlight.

I am having such a bad weekend of running into obstacles. Fate sure is testing me.

The wall feels cold and rough. Ah a door, it creaked as I opened it. Found a light switch to the left of the door.

A lab with lots of beautiful rocks. I sat down at the table in the middle of the room covered with notebooks and microscopes. Everything was dusty indicating no one had been in here for awhile. A purple rock caught my eye, I picked it up trying to remember where I had seen a similar one. It is way bigger than any of the ones I have. Why does it look familiar?

A water spout. Yes, some water, it better be good. I forgot to fill up my canteen. It tasted like the spring water at the pond. Tummy grumbled again. Looking all around no other door no other way to escape. Foohey.

I flipped through the pages of a journal while devouring the peaches. Lots of formulas and notes. I did ok in chemistry but that was also seven years ago. None of it makes sense to me.

I wonder if the guys have been back to the library. I giggled thinking about them not finding me. Score one for team Annie. I could use a bathroom. I walked behind another row of shelves, flipped another light on, saw a small door hidden in the corner.

A small room with a bucket, waterfall shower like the one this morning, and a rock formation. I am not going in the bucket, gross. Rock formation, this morning there was a similar one but it had a lid with a hole under it. My guess an endless hole you do not want to explore. I assume their answer to an outhouse. Plus side on endless hole, the smell is not there like an outhouse. I hate those things. It is better than the bucket option.

I continued reading for a few hours according to my watch. I never leave home without it. I think I better head back. The only way to get home. I stuffed several books into my backpack, turned the lights off. Took one last look at the large purple rock.

The photo in the cottage!

That is where I saw it. Should I take it with me? What if they want to look in my backpack since I had been gone for so long? I think if they knew about this place they would be here by now. I will leave it and come back down again with Dorie. I hope she will want to. She is not real adventurous.

Back down the short tunnel grinning about my secret. I wonder if that is what Damien is searching for. I am one step ahead of you.

I opened the door slowly so I could peek out. I did not see anyone. Odd. I decided I would grab a book and lay down on the floor behind a bookcase. Pretend I fell asleep. Men are terrible about looking all over. I am sure they will not look here.

TWELVE

"I want it back." The white ghost whispered into my ear.

I was too terrified to get up off the floor of the library. I prayed the guys would walk in now. Hoping it would scare Ms. Scary away. I closed my eyes pretending I did not hear her. Please go away. I take back wanting to know a ghost.

"I want it back." I opened my eyes and she was directly above my face. My heart stopped. She flew to the rock section of the bookshelves. She kept flying back and forth. It created enough breeze that a book fell to the floor. I crawled over and saw the picture of the purple rock. No, she can not be trying to tell me she wants the rock. Why does everyone want that rock? I have got to found out what is special about it. Sorry ghost I am not giving it to you.

The front door swung open. I jumped up. It was Brad looking upset.

"Where the heck were you? We have been looking for the past hour."

"I was reading one of the books over there and fell asleep. Did you see the ghost again?"

He shook his head. He looked where I pointed. I do not think he believed me but he did not say anymore.

"It is time to go back home. Damian left awhile ago. He had no patience for finding you."

"What about the other buildings? There is one more to look at on this side and then the other side."

"Oh, they are sleeping quarters, living spaces. We checked them out. Nothing interesting, mostly empty other than a few furnishings."

I wish I could tell Brad about the lab so I could grab that rock. I wonder why the ghost does not show up in the tunnels? Interesting. Maybe the lab is the better place for the rock. I can not wait to talk to Dorie. She will come down with me. I am not coming here alone.

We headed back to the cottage. I was very happy to see that ladder leading up.

"I guess there is no other way in but this way?" I asked stepping up on the ladder rungs.

"No."

"But, how did Damian get down here? The door was locked from our side."

"I did not bother to ask. You ask to many questions."

"You leave room for so many questions."

He motioned for me to keep climbing and did not say another word until we were inside the cottage in the kitchen.

"I am ready for some real food. How about a couple sandwiches before we head to town?"

I shook my head yes. My watch read 3:00. It seemed like an eternity down there. I have to admit the most exciting weekend I have had since graduation. When Dorie and I go back down it will be for a day with plenty of snacks.

Brad brought the sandwiches to the table along with a bottle of Pepsi. I grinned a great big smile. I reached for it but he pulled it away.

"Forgive me?"

"No."

"I deserve that. How about truths for now." He held out the Pepsi.

I can live with that for awhile. I took it and chugged it. I must bring Pepsis with those snacks next time. The sun shone through the kitchen window warming my face.

"I missed sunshine. How do you think the people survived with no light?" I asked.

"Good question. There was some light. It could be we only found a part of the town. Maybe there is a whole different part that has sunshine and green grass." He said. His eyes sparkled when he smiled.

Charming, the reason I need to be away from him. No time for that even if it was fun. I do miss having a boyfriend. I am not sure about the trust thing. Brad has proven to not be trusted. It will take a lot to gain my trust after this weekend. I hope Damian stays away.

"We better start walking back to town. It is a bit of a distance."

"No car?" I asked.

"No road. My car is at my office building."

It was a beautiful walk back to town. The birds were chirping. The silence between us was golden.

THIRTEEN

I fell on to my comfy bed. A relief to be home after a long weekend. I wish I did not have to work tomorrow, I would sleep all day curled up under the covers. My eyes closed welcoming dreamland.

I woke up smelling a heavenly smell. The clock on my wall read six o'clock. I bolted out of bed heading for the kitchen. Brad was cooking bacon and eggs. He smiled at me as I sat down at the table.

"Hello, did you have a nice nap? I went in to say goodbye and you were out. I didn't want to leave with things unsaid so I took a nap. Guess we were both tired. This is all you had in the fridge for supper." he said placing my plate in front of me.

"Thank you. I'm surprised I had anything in the fridge. I normally hit the store on the weekend for the week's supply." The eggs were wonderful but were missing something, ketchup. I grabbed the ketchup out of the fridge and squirted some on them. Brad looked at me funny.

"My dad showed me this when I was a little girl. It is yummy, try it."

He shook his head no. If someone walked in now, they would think we were starved animals the way we shoveled the food in our mouths.

"Why did you lie?" I asked.

"I know I did wrong by not being truthful and I hope to make it up. Starting with my fabulous cooking." he smiled.

"You are avoiding the question."

"I honestly don't know why I went along with Damian. Simple as that. Nothing to tell. I'm sorry."

Way to avoid. I'll figure it out.

"Thanks for the food, the adventure, and bringing my ex back into my life but I would really like some alone time before I work tomorrow." I placed my plate in the sink.

"Ok. Maybe I will swing by the store tomorrow."

I didn't say anything. He left. I can breathe again.

Turned the TV on and flipped through the channels not paying attention. My mind on him. I don't think he plans on leaving me alone. Not sure I like it. I have been so use to being alone that I don't know if I want someone constantly there. I feel smothered.

I thought about calling Damian's wife and telling her about the weekend. I'm sure that would put a stop to him bothering me for awhile. She rules the roost. I have to admit he has my curiosity in full force, dang it. I will play along for awhile.

I did call my best friend, Dorie and told her everything. She dropped her phone at one moment from the shock. She thinks I am nuts to go along with whatever Damian wants. She never did like him. She did say she would go down there with me. That surprised me, I thought I would have to beg. That sparked energy to pack my backpack with all the things we will need this weekend. I am not going unprepared. First thing in the pack was my digital camera for proof to show my grandparents. They are not getting out of telling me what they know.

FOURTEEN

I decided on a new outfit I bought last week for work. A buttoned up blue blouse, grey mini skirt, and blue flats for shoes. I added jewelry, styled my hair, and put make-up on. Looking in the mirror, I looked pretty good. I had not dressed up in quite awhile. I am pleased to say I have not gained any weight since high school. Flat tummy, full boobs, and curves in the right places. Now, if I had a bit of height, short changed on that one. I don't wear heels to add height because I would break my ankle in a heart beat.

After unlocking the shop, I found a note from dad saying it was a slow weekend so he was able to mark all the merchandise and stock the shelves. He left the list out for me to see the new items. Normally, I would be bored today but this will give me time to research my rock collection that is in the display window. I have several purple ones and I brought the notebooks I found.

I headed to the back office.

Flipped open the lab book I had and began reading the scribbled notes on the rock study. It was mostly foreign to me. Guess that is why there are libraries full of information I can look up to figure this out.

I have always loved rocks and collected one from each trip we took as a family. But I never did any deep research on them. I like the way they sparkle. It is my second largest collection, first being my books of course. The third collection is teddy bears. I have stuffed ones, ceramic ones, and knick knack ones. Dad is going to have to build me some shelves soon, running out of room.

I know dad has a few books on rocks here in the shop. He was the one to spark my interest in them. I bet he would know about these purple rocks but I am not ready to ask questions yet. I need to find out a few things first. Then he better be truthful this time. I can not believe my parents are mixed up in this mystery. I thought they were normal uneventful people. It is exciting but surprising.

The first book I found had a picture of my purple rock. The rock is called a Purthyst. A crystal widely found in the ground. The deeper color of purple the more expensive and higher energy. The rock is known to calm emotions and clear the mind. It is thought to strengthen the immune system.

Interesting, but why does Damian want one so badly. If they are easily found, he could find his own. I picked up the deepest purple rock and examined it from all angles. It is beautiful.

"Why are you special?" I spoke out loud.

"Well, I am handsome, charming, and available." Brad said leaning against the door frame.

I dropped the rock onto the floor.

"Do not do that! What the heck!" Bending down picking up the rock.

"Sorry. You should have a buzzer on your front door so people don't scare you or rob you."

"I'll make a note of that, but people around here are trustworthy and like family so never has been a need for one. Normally, someone announces themselves. Are you trying to spy?"

"Now, why would I do that."

Smart ass.

"I was on my way to my shop, when I thought I would ask if you would go out to dinner with me tonight?" Brad asked.

"Um, I think I want to stay home tonight. Still tired." He is like a disease you can't get rid of. Good grief.

"Ok, maybe another time. This time I will leave. Quite the rock. My Aunt had several of them around her house here. I was hoping to take you over there. She said they were magical."

"Oh, your Aunt's house? I didn't know you had an Aunt from here."

"I didn't mention that. Must have slipped my mind with everything going on in the tunnels."

"Who is this Aunt? What house in town?"

"I will tell all when you agree to a supper. In fact, I will cook it at my Aunt's house."

"I think you are a con artist and not an accountant."

He grinned.

"How about tomorrow. Call me with details."

"I need your number." He grinned his charming smile. I wrote the store number down. I am here more than home. I followed him out and watched him cross the street to his office building.

It is things like that which make me curious about him. He is quite the actor. One minute, I think he knows nothing about all this mystery then the next he hints enough to reel me in.

"Well played Mr. Brad."

"Brad who?" Said my mom standing behind me. I jumped a bit. A habit lately.

"What is with people scaring me today?"

"I was not quiet. I came through the back door. I wanted to see how you are doing. I missed hearing from you this weekend. Where did you go?"

My mom the curious, sweet, and short as me lady. Even though I disappear on weekends, she still has to call to talk to me at least once. I have a cellphone but I am not in the habit of taking it everywhere. I like to disappear from it as well as everyone. Which reminds me I need to figure out where I left it at home.

"I spent a lot of time at the creek reading. Sorry." I gave her a kiss on the cheek.

"You are going to turn into a book. Now, who is Brad? Anyone special?" She grinned.

"No, he is the accountant across the street. He popped in to say hi and introduce himself."

I started to dust the shelves hoping she would drop the subject. No such luck.

"Is he single? What is his last name? Did he ask you out?"

"Mother!" Banging my head on the shelf from frustration. She needs to stop!

"Quit that! You will give yourself a headache."

"At this moment I prefer the headache to your match making!"

"Dear, I am your mother I have every right to. I will not stop until you are happily married. Ever since that Damien guy you live like a nun. You are my only daughter and I look forward to your wedding day. I will not stop. My duty as a mom. Get over it."

Mom has some spunk.

"His name is Brad Stanford and yes he asked me to dinner."

No reply. I turned around, she looked as white as Ms. Scary ghost.

"Mom, are you ok?"

"Sure." she said quietly. She walked to the back and I heard the door slam.

My mom does not slam doors. What is going on?

After work, went home, sat thinking about how they could know each other. I fell asleep.

FIFTEEN

I quickly sat up. I looked around the living room and there sat Damien on the loveseat. I forgot to lock the door when I got home. My front door is squeaky, how did I not hear that. It was an exhausting day with mom and Brad.

"Hi sunshine!" He said.

"What are you doing here? I did not invite you over."

"Well, the wife was not happy that I spoke to you this weekend so she kicked me out."

"And your first thought was to come here?"

"You are on the way to my parents. When you did not answer your door I figured you were ignoring me. It was unlocked, you should lock it."

"You should NOT come on in!" My blood was boiling.

"Oh, calm down. I wanted to discuss the weekend without everyone around. Do you have something to drink? I am thirsty."

"No, this is not a tea party."

"Such anger. Anger is not healthy for the soul or body. Lighten up."

"Um, you are married, we have a history, and you have me involved in something I do not understand. Leave now."

"No can do yet. I am warning you to stay away from Brad in the romantic way. He is not who you think he is."

"Let's see. It is you who brought us back together. It is none of your business what I do in that department of my life. I get enough meddling from my mom. No room for you too."

"I miss your mom. Such a sweet lady. But seriously, Brad was suppose to get you to the cave not get romantic. "

"Why was he to get me to the cave? Why all the secrecy?"

"I knew you would not have went with me. I remember you meeting him, so when I ran into him it was the right place at the right time. I thought if you were on an adventure you would spill more knowledge being caught up in the fun. I feel a bit of hostility towards me so I knew you would not answer my questions."

"You think! It could not be that you cheated on me with your wife that caused the hostility."

"Now, that is not the way I remember it."

"Whatever. Now, tell me what is so special about the cave."

"In due time. I have faith your curiosity will discover it all for me."

"You do not know either." I laughed.

He walked to the door.

"Honey, I know way more than you. It will blow your mind. I can not wait. Sweet revenge for breaking my heart." He winked.

"Your heart! Just leave. Do not come back!" I pushed him out the door and slammed it.

The tears fell. Why do I let him get to me? It has been over for seven years. I am pathetic. I need to get my mind off this whole situation. If I was a runner, I would run, but I think a big bowl of ice cream will help. And a funny movie.

An hour later, a stomach full of chocolate chip ice cream, and half way through the Three Stooges I fell asleep on the couch. No dreams of Damien.

I awoke to Brad sitting on the edge of my couch staring at me. This is getting too creepy.

"Whoa. How long have you been sitting there?" I asked.

"Long enough to watch the drool fall off your chin." He grinned. I wiped my chin, how embarrassing.

"Why are you here?" I forgot to lock the door again.

"Your mom came to see me. She told me she saw Damien's car here and thought I might rescue you."

"Mom? What time is it?"

"Midnight."

"I thought it was morning at first. Why did my mom come see you?"

"She was curious about me. I think she wants us to date, so I went along with it. Nice lady."

"She goes too far at times. When I told her your full name she looked white as a ghost. Why? Who are you that she would know?"

"I do not know. We talked about my business and Carl's farm. Why was Damien here?"

"He was being a butt as usual. He did not stay long. Sometimes living in a small town is a curse when your parents live close by."

I get the feeling more secrets are being kept. Weird that they are between my mom and Brad.

"Have you read the journal you found in the cave?" He asked.

"No, I have not had time with all my visitors showing up lately." I said sarcastically. I yawned.

"I'll let you sleep. I promise to not show up without being invited." I followed him to the front door.

"Good night." I said waiting in the doorway to watch him walk away. Very strange week. I made sure to lock the door. Dreamland came quickly.

I awoke tired from the emotional day before. Mom shows up today I am telling her to butt out of my social life. I need peace from one of them. I do not think Brad is going to go away until all this is figured out.

What the heck could blow my mind away?

The store was rather busy. It was nice because it gave me less time to think about past days. No mom or Brad thank goodness.

Normal day finally.

SIXTEEN

After work, I headed to my grandparents' house. I could see that my mom's car was still at home which will give me alone time with grandpa before she takes him grocery shopping. My grandparents do not like to drive anymore so we take turns taking them places. I opened the side door that led to the kitchen. Grandpa was eating a snack.

"What do I owe this surprise for?" He asked smiling.

"I have questions about the history of Obeyville. I figured you were the perfect person." I sat down next to him.

"I will try to answer. The mind does not remember sometimes." He winked.

"What do you know about the cave under the town?" I watched his facial expression turn to shock. He stopped eating and leaned back in his chair.

"It is a myth."

"Um, no it is not. I was down there last weekend."

"Seriously? I thought it was a myth."

"There is a whole town plus a pond with a waterfall. It is exciting and beautiful. I came across a hidden room off the library that looked like a lab with notebooks and rocks."

"Who have you told?"

"No one."

"I would not bother. I doubt anyone would believe you. I am not convinced, I know how you like to read those fantasy books."

Grandpa is stubborn. He is not taking the bait. I will take my camera this weekend and once I show him the pictures he will have to talk. I kissed him on the cheek and left. His reaction tells me he knows what I am talking about.

Brad was parked in my drive when I got there. Good grief, what happened to being invited.

"I decided to invite you for dinner. I am still unpacking if you do not mind the mess." He said.

"I thought you were going to call the store?"

"You did not give me your personal number therefore I had to come by to invite you over." Sneaky.

"What night?" I want to see this Aunt's place. Look for those rocks.

"Today is Tuesday, how about tomorrow at my Aunt's since we will be heading back to the cave on Friday?"

"Sure. I thought you stayed at the cottage."

"Not during the week. My Aunt's was given to me and has been in the family forever. It is across town. I will pick you up about six?"

"Make it seven. I close the shop at six and that will give me time to get ready. Dress or casual?"

"Casual will be fine. See you then." He winked and drove off.

Finally a quiet night at home. I remembered to lock the door. No unwanted visitors tonight. I made a sandwich, grabbed the journal, and flopped down on the couch. Glad I will be able to read a bit of it before Friday.

The journal was boring until the second month of entries. I bolted straight up off the couch. I have to go back to grandpa's. This journal is proof! He can not avoid the question now.

I was surprised to see the lights still on. I knocked on the door since it was evening time. I did not want to surprise them. The door opened, it was Brad! What the hell!

"Why are you here? How do you know my grandparents?" I asked angrily storming past him.

"Oh, boy, here we go." Brad followed me to the kitchen.

"How do you know Brad?" I asked my grandparents. They looked at me then to Brad.

"His grandpa was a friend in high school. We were catching up on old memories he told Brad about. I did not realize the two of you knew each other." Grandpa was fiddling with his coffee cup.

"Why did you not tell me you knew grandpa?" I asked Brad.

"You did not ask."

"I think it was a given since we talked about things last weekend. I do not understand all the secrets around here."

Brad did not look at me. I opened up the journal to the page with grandma's name on it. He grinned.

"Explain. There is now proof you know about the cave. Who is this lady, Sonja? She talks like grandma is the other woman and that you are Sonja's boyfriend. Please someone explain." I pointed at the faded name on the page.

"Sonja owned the local jewelry store. We were engaged to be married. She was the expert on the rocks and I did the mining work. Brad's grandpa and I were recruited to mine right out of high school. We became close working and living down there. Pretty neat place, huh? Bob dated your grandma at the time I was with Sonja." Grandma winked at grandpa.

Wow, I never thought about them two being with anyone but each other. They never talked about other dates.

"Your grandma was the cook in the restaurant. I met her the first morning during breakfast and I could not take my eyes off her. She was the most beautiful thing and smiled all the time. Then I found out she was with Bob and I was with Sonja. It was expected that I marry Sonja. Her mom was my mom's best friend and next door neighbor. We grew up together. We were the best of friends. Your grandma was not from around here."

"I am beyond shocked. Why did you not say something before at family gatherings? Does mom know?" I asked.

"No, she does not. One did not talk about relationships openly like you kids do. Bob moved away after things went sour with your grandma and him. No it was not my fault. I happened to see Brad come out of his office today and knew I had seen him before. He resembles Bob. We talked and I invited him over for a drink. I wanted to catch up on the whereabouts of his grandpa."

"Sonja was not blind to your feelings for grandma, it is in the journal. What about the purple rocks?"

"It has something to do with a new energy source. Sonja did not tell me all the details, by then we were not on speaking terms. She left in a big hurry and no one knows why. The cave was shut down and everyone was told to forget about it. In fact, we were threatened to say we knew nothing about it."

"This is so crazy. A mystery right under our feet."

"If you must keep looking into it, I can not stop you. Please do not say anything to your mom until we can. She thinks we are innocent." He winked at grandma.

I hugged him and agreed. I need more information anyway. Brad remained at grandpa's. I was glad he did not follow me out. He probably knew I would be angry for leaving details out about his Aunt and my grandpa.

Jerk.

I will make him answer tomorrow. I began reading more of the journal. My eyes kept closing. I remembered that I talked about the lab, crap, Brad knows about it now. Energy rocks would make them valuable.

Think Damien was gloating about my grandparents not being together back then. He knows how I loved the fact that they were soul mates and saved themselves for one another. He would get a kick out of that but that seems mild.

There is something else.

SEVENTEEN

Dorie showed up at the shop the next day.

"This is a nice surprise. What are you doing here?" I asked.

"I got the feeling my bestie was needing a hug." She hugged me.

"My grandpa called you, didn't he?" I asked sarcastically.

She shook her head yes.

"Tell me what is going on with this Brad man?"

"You have met Brad before. The summer after we graduated the bonfire. We picked him up from Carl Wilson's farm."

"I remember the party. I think I would have to see him. Too many guys there that night and we were definitely plowed. Oh, good times. I believe that was the last time I saw you with a guy. Kind of weird it is the same guy to bring you out of your nun hood." She laughed.

She knows my mom calls me a nun.

"I like being picky after the crap with Damien."

"I do not blame you. I think your heart has not mended from him."

I shook my head in agreement. She has a valid point. It is never good to start another relationship if you are not over the previous. Maybe deep down I knew that so I never was interested anyone else until now.

"I hope this date tonight fills in some of the mystery about him. I have to admit last weekend was exciting. Are you staying through this weekend?"

"Yes I am. I needed a break from school. I can not wait to graduate. Tired of studying."

"Good, you will love what I have to show you down there."

I filled her in on all the details for the weekend.

Dorie headed home and I locked the store up for the day. I climbed in the tub when I got home. The best stress releaser there is. I must have dozed off because I heard the front doorbell ring. I baled out of the tub pulling my robe on.

I opened the front door and it was Brad. He looked me up and down then smiled.

"A bit more casual than I intended but I will take it." He said joking around.

"I fell asleep in the tub, I guess it relaxed me too much. I will be ready in a few." I motioned for him to sit on the couch.

I opened my closet pulled out a cute little black mini skirt with a simple plain red T-shirt. I little bit sexy but casual. When I walked out he smiled approvingly of the outfit.

We drove across town, then down a dirt road that led about three miles out of town. Around the bend an old colonial house stood. The most beautiful thing. How did I not know this was here.

"Impressive." I said.

"This has been in the family since the town began. My Aunt lived in it last on my dad's side. I did unpack the kitchen today but excuse the rest of the boxes. I have been preoccupied this week." He smiled at me.

Parked the car and walked up the five steps that led to the front double doors. I loved the large wrap around porch like you see in a country home magazine. The door opened to a large foyer with a table in the center. There were sheets covering the wall hangings and the furniture along with boxes against the walls. Two staircases leading to the second floor. He led me down a hallway with several small rooms off it. We ended up in a large kitchen that made mine look like a hole in the wall. The appliances were old and along with the rest of the kitchen. It needed an update but still a grand kitchen. I would take it.

"I do need to upgrade. Do you know a good designer?" He asked.

"No, you have seen my outdated kitchen. I need one too."

He began taking food out of the fridge and placing it on the table in front of me. He went all out on the meal. I could get use to this. I do alright cooking just sucks cooking for one. I tend to get lazy and eat sandwiches a lot.

"It is fun to cook for someone. One person, the food goes to waste." Brad said reading my mind.

"I agree."

He grabbed a bottle of wine, two glasses, and poured us some. A nice drink with supper.

"Tell me about you and this house." I said sipping my wine.

"My Aunt passed away a year ago and left me the house. She thought since I helped Carl out I might appreciate it more than any other family member. Plus, I am her favorite." He grinned.

"Of course you are. Sorry to hear about her passing. Where are your parents?"

They are divorced. Dad lives out East somewhere. He has not been a part of my life since I was five. I grew up in California with my mom. My Aunt visited us numerous times when she could. She was spunky for an older lady. Aunt Sonja is grandpa Bob's sister. Bob is my dad's father. He was angry that dad left us like he did. I was fortunate that my mom allowed the rest of the family to still be a part of our life. Lot of my friends who had nasty divorces could no longer see their other side. My mom did not judge. Grandpa Bob adored her and said his son was stupid to let her go. I was surprised when your grandpa said he was to marry Aunt Sonja, nothing was ever said about her ever dating. We called her the old maid in the family, even she called herself that. She was fun. I miss her."

"Amazing the secrets families' keep. I love the house and your Aunt sounds fun. Do I get a tour after eating?"

"You bet. Just excuse the dust and the clutter."

"I bet this house could tell a few more secrets." I said watching his reaction. He seemed to tense up a bit.

"Have you read more of my Aunt's journal?" He avoided the comment.

"I was too tired last night. I fell asleep with it wide open." He laughed.

"Did I see your friend at the shop today?" He asked.

"Yes." I said wondering how did he know.

"My office is across the street."

I swear he can read my thoughts at times. I know it is across the street but how long was he watching. My own stalker. Hopefully, a good stalker, if there is one.

"Let's take a tour of this fabulous old home." Brad said putting his dishes in the sink.

"I think you will love this room the most." Brad opened the doors to a magnificent library.

I pointed to the woodwork.

"It looks like the same wood design as the one in the cave library." I said stunned.

"Yes, it is. My Aunt had the same artisan do both."

"Why did you not say so?"

"What fun would that be? Plus, I did not want Damien to know my connection to the cave. I do not trust him either. There are some questions I want answered and he may be able to do that."

"I knew it. Well played though. So, do you know about the lab?"

"The hidden lab? Yes. Damien no. That is where you were when I could not find you, correct."

I smiled. Maybe I can trust Brad. Time will tell.

"You are welcome to read any of the books here. Watch out for the dust at first. It has been a year since anyone lived here."

"I thought Grandpa said Sonja left before him and grandma were dating."

I'm confused.

"Oh, she was not the last occupant here. I have another Aunt. She liked to keep to herself. I doubt your grandpa knew her. She had a maid and butler do all her errands. She rarely left the house. When she did she made a point of going out of town. Never understood her."

"Sounds like another family secret." I said.

"Maybe. I will show you upstairs, follow me."

He seems to change the subject when there is something he does not want me to know about or ask more questions. Maybe I should offer to clean for him and do some snooping around. Old houses tend to tell a lot if you know where to look. I see lots of possible answers hidden within these walls.

The upstairs had four bedrooms and a bathroom. The rooms were small but had character. Everything was covered with white sheets. I thought that was only in movies people covered their furniture. We headed back downstairs.

"I thought there is a third floor. I saw it when driving up."

"There is but I have not found the key to unlock the door to it. I do not want to break the door. They are too neat to break. I think it is a large ballroom up there."

"I would like to see that."

"Once I find the key. I am sure there are more valuables up there and maybe a secret or two." He winked.

I like when he winks at me. Makes the butterflies in my tummy fly.

"I could clean for you in exchange for some good home cooked meals at night." I said trying to persuade him. I can be snooping around plus get my mom to stop trying to set me up. I bet Mom will watch the shop in the afternoon just because it is for Brad. A win situation. Plus, I love his cooking.

"I think that is a great idea. I need it cleaned and I hate eating alone."

"I will start next Monday afternoon."

I could not stop smiling on the drive to my house. I bet there are plenty of family secrets to uncover. Brad walked me to the door. He kissed me on the cheek which surprised me.

"I had a great first date. Thank you." Brad said.

"Yes, I did too. Or is it our second date? Remember years ago we had one."

"That one doesn't count since you don't recall it. Therefore, this is the first date. A much better first date with good food and conversation." He smiled.

I kissed him on the lips. I couldn't resist after those sweet words.

"Good night. Sweet dreams." I turned to open my door and stepped in.

I watched him walk to his car. I locked the dang door. I am not forgetting tonight. Especially, with hormones raging. Moderation is key. Baby steps in this relationship. Learn from past mistakes.

EIGHTEEN

The day is here to explore the cave again. I know Dorie will like it. The day seemed to drag at the store from being anxious to find more information in the cave. I rushed home after locking up the store and ate a quick bite while packing sandwiches to take. This adventure was going to have plenty of real food and no canned fruits. I grabbed a couple Pepsis for my daily sugar rush. I bought three new flashlights with new batteries. I packed plenty of change of clothes along with a jacket. I sat down on the couch to wait for my fellow adventurers. Dorie was the first to arrive.

"I could not sleep last night thinking about this." Dorie said checking her backpack again.

"Did you bring a jacket?" I asked. She shook her head no. I gave her one from my closet.

"Thanks, I completely forgot it laying on my bed. My mom would not stop asking where we were going. I fibbed a bit and said we were going camping. Hopefully, she does not remember how much I hate camping. The whole bugs and using an outhouse thing.

"Thanks. Until we know details I would like it between us. No need to worry our parents. Parents are notorious for reacting. The more we know the better before we explain it all."

A knock at the door turned out to be Brad.

"Hi there." Brad said reaching to shake Dorie's hand.

"Hi back." Dorie was looking googly eye at him. She could not stop staring. I had to nudge her to get her back to reality. She grinned an approving smile at me.

We walked to Brad's cottage in silence. A beautiful Spring afternoon with little wind and plenty of sunshine. It is amazing that all these years his cottage was right here. I noticed this time that there was a lot of brush surrounding it. I suppose it could be easily missed. I never reached this far in the woods. It is strange that my friends had never said anything when they explored this far. One of them was Damien. I'm learning I did not know him as well as I thought.

Brad unlocked his door and we sat down at the table for a small break.

"Have a snack while we catch our breathe. Did you pack something other than canned fruit?" Brad asked chuckling at me.

"I sure did. I have ham sandwiches and snack bars."

"No Pepsi?" Brad teased.

"Oh, yes. I would not forget that."

Dorie watched us banter back and forth. I saw the look in her eye that told me she liked us together. I do enjoy Brad's company. Maybe it has been long enough sulking over Damien. Heck he has been married for those seven years. He obviously got over me.

"I say let's get going." I said feeling anxious to show Dorie the cave.

We climbed down the ladder to the open room with the trunks. I searched the biggest trunk for any new information. It was mostly tools for mining. I was hoping for some books or journals.

"Hey, I think I have a map." Brad said unfolding a worn out piece of paper on to the long table against the wall.

All of us shone our flashlights on it. It looked like a map of the town with more tunnels branching off from it. Lots more exploring to do. The name Cruze Mining at the bottom of the paper. Dorie and I looked at each other shocked. That is Damien's last name.

"All these years knowing Damien, he never mentioned this place. I can not believe he kept it a secret from me. We were best friends. I told him everything." I said feeling hurt.

Dorie touched my arm reassuring me that she was there for me.

"Sometimes secrets are meant to stay secrets. He may have a good reason for never telling you." Brad said.

I shot him a dirty look. Now he is defending him.

"Men!" Dorie exclaimed reading my thoughts.

"I do not see any other entrances but your cottage." I said.

"The map looks like it is meant to continue the way it ends at the edge." Brad said pointing to the edge.

It did look like it was tore.

"There must be another map somewhere. I can not see that there is only one entrance with all these tunnels."

"Possibly why the map is tore, another entrance that someone does not want known." Brad said.

"Now that I know the way to your cottage I can see the layout in proportion with the cave here. If I trace in my mind both, it seems the end that is torn leads to under the downtown. Interesting." I said.

"Definitely, need to find the other half." Brad said walking towards the tunnel leading to the pond and town of buildings.

Dorie stopped when we reached the waterfall.

"This is magnificent! I have to swim a bit." Dorie tore off her clothes revealing a swim suit. I was holding my breathe for a minute there. I did not think to tell her to bring one. She waded in and swam to the middle of the pond. I followed by stripping and revealing my swim suit. I was prepared this time.

"Was I the only one who did not think to bring a swim suit? Dang." Brad said sitting down on a rock and watching us. He looked disappointed. Thank goodness he did not strip and go naked. I kind of thought he would. He surprised me.

"This is better than you described Annie." Dorie said floating on her back.

"Yep. I need one in my backyard." I said. We swam for about twenty minutes.

"Time to get back to exploring. Lots of ground to cover." Brad said standing up starting for the storage room before the tunnel. We caught up to him. We searched the trunks in there but no map. Where could it be? I hope the person did not keep it that tore it.

"I hope you remembered the key." I said to Brad.

"I might have forgotten a suit, but I did remember the key." He winked at me.

I grabbed a couple more journals from the trunks. I have a little bit more to read from the last one but will be ready for these. They are beginning to be interesting especially with my grandparents involved.

It was chilly walking through the tunnel with a wet suit on under my clothes.

"Now I know why I forgot my suit." said Brad hearing my teeth clatter. Such a funny guy.

Dorie and I sat down at the table outside of the Saloon building.

"I will run down to the power room to turn the electricity on." Brad said leaving us alone. Damien must have shown him the power room when I was exploring the lab. Funny he never said anything and we left the power on when we left last time.

"Extrordinary, isn't it?" I asked Dorie.

"That is the understatement. To think it was down here all the time we were growing up. I am amazed."

The lights came on. I had not noticed the beautiful stone work on the outside of the buildings last weekend. A stone I need to research. I might like to add it to my house.

"Did you see the street lights?" Brad asked when he got to the table.

"They are lights." I said thinking he was making fun of me.

"Look close."

I walked over to one. They are the purple rocks!

"How are they not glowing purple?" I asked.

"Not sure on that one, but I bet Aunt Sonja discovered how to create the energy out of them. I bet Damien discovered this from his family since they were the mining company."

"But why involve us?" I asked frustrated with this mystery.

"Maybe because your grandpa mined them which means he knows where plenty of them are. My Aunt knew the science so he got me involved. He knew you would not confide in him but perhaps you would with me if I got to know you. I think him seeing you and I in the Spa ignited a bit of jealousy too."

"No, he was being selfish. He did not want me but he did not want anyone else to have me either."

"Finally! You see the real him." Dorie said walking towards the library. She thought I was a fool for loving him. She said he was bad news. I did not want to believe it. I do now.

We followed Dorie.

"Why are you going there?" I asked Dorie.

"I think I saw something looking out of the window."

Brad and I looked at each other. I mouthed our ghost.

The books were everywhere on the floor. It looked like a tornado had passed through. I began picking them up placing them back on the shelf.

"Thumb through the pages first for the other half of the map." Brad said helping me.

"Good idea."

"A beautiful room. I see why you talked so much about it." Dorie said walking to the other side of the room away from us.

"Did you tell her about Ms. Scary?" Brad asked whispering.

"No, she would freak."

"Ok. Why would a ghost throw the books?"

"Last time I ran into her, she made the book of rocks fall onto the floor with the purple rock showing. I think she wants the rock." I said.

"But she is a ghost!"

"I did not say it made sense. In fact, none of this does."

Dorie began jumping up and down waving a piece of paper. We ran over as she spread it out on to a table.

The other half of the map! Thank you Ms. Scary.

"Look you are correct, it is the business side of the town above ground. The arrows point up in each store on your side of the street."

"I do not know how my store would have an opening. There is nothing there."

"I bet your grandpa covered it up. Mine was hidden good."

"True."

"You could ask your grandpa." Dorie said.

"I do evidence of it, but I think I will wait until we find out more answers. He hid the truth for some reason. I think some of it might be in those journals." I said.

"I am disappointed no openings on my side of the street." Brad said frowning.

"I can share mine with you." Teasing him.

"How do you get into the secret room?" Brad asked.

I walked to the bookshelf pulled the book down and the door opened.

"Awesome!" Dorie clapped her hands entering the door. I am surprised how excited she is about this. She loves fun but was never one for adventures.

We reached the lab. I showed the lab book to Dorie. She started flipping through it. She was smiling.

"You are not going to believe this!" She said holding up the book pointing to one of the formulas.

"What?" I asked.

"It is a formula for time travel! Fricken time travel!" She exclaimed grinning from ear to ear.

"That is not possible. Those are stories, fantasies." I said.

"They figured it out. Looks like your purple rock is a source for time travel. This diagram is a machine and this is showing how many ounces the rock needs to be to run it." Dorie pointed to the diagram.

"You know nothing about Chemistry and Science. You hated it in school." I was stumped how she could know anything about it.

"Um, I changed my major this semester. It was boring all the business classes. I took a Chemistry class to see if I would like it. I loved it. I understood it. Science is my new major just not sure what direction I want to take with it."

I was shocked.

"Maybe I should have done that. I agree business classes are boring." Brad said.

"My new lab partner, Ned, is studying to be a gemologist. I wonder if he would help us out with this. His family owns a jewelry store." Dorie said with a smile. I see a hint of love possibly.

"Whoa, we do not need a lot of people knowing about this yet. If there really is a time machine, that is huge news and we need to keep it between us." Brad said interrupting us.

"True. Do you think the machine is built?" I asked getting excited.

"There are more buildings we had not explored on the other side. We can try there." Brad said heading that way. No wonder Damien was interested. Big money to the right person, not to mention history!

NINETEEN

I flipped the lights on in the building to reveal a massive living room area with several couches and chairs. There was a door to the right which ended up being a bathroom. I headed upstairs where there were beds and a couple more bathrooms. It was all basic living quarters, nothing fancy or personal. Rather boring. I headed back downstairs.

Dorie was staring at a picture on the wall. It was the same purple stone on the beach picture like at Brad's cottage.

"Where did Brad go?" I asked her.

"He went to the next building hoping to find the time machine."

"That is the same photo hanging at Brad's cottage." I said sitting down on the sofa across from it. Dorie joined me on the couch. We were mesmorized by the photo.

"He knows more than he is telling us." I said. Dorie grabbed my arm shaking it.

"What do you want, I am right here." She pointed towards the front door. Ms. Scary is back.

"I want it back." Ms. Scary said.

"You keep saying that. I do not know what it is." I said.

Ms. Scary flew to the photo we had been staring at before she showed up. The second time she has showed me a purple rock. She vanished when Brad opened the door.

"I found a machine that I am assuming is a time travel one. The next building." He motioned for us to follow.

The ghost reappeared flying around us in circles before we got to the door. It stopped in front of Brad poking it's ghostly finger at him.

"I want it back, NOW!" Ms. Scary repeated again. Brad looked confused.

"I have no clue to what you want." Brad said.

"I think the purple stone." I said pointing to the photo.

"That looks like the exact photo in my cottage. You are dead, no stone will help you." He yelled at Ms. Scary.

She did not like that. She screeched like the time before and vanished through the wall to the other building.

We ran next door. She was frantically flying about. We had to duck several times.

"Where is the machine?" I asked.

Brad led us upstairs where a huge machine in the middle of the room stood. The ghost was pointing to it. The stone and the machine must be connected and Ms. Scary knows that.

"Who are you? What do you know about this machine?" I asked. She flew to Brad who had a confused look on his face.

"What are you not telling us, Brad?" I asked angrily.

"Nothing. I do not know why she is flying around me." He was getting mad now.

The ghost stood beside Brad and became more clear in features. It was like watching the focus on a camera. Brad's eyes grew big from shock.

"Aunt Sophia!" he said.

The ghost smiled for once.

"Why did you not show yourself before?" He asked.

"Because I wanted you to stop searching. This project is dangerous."

"Project?" I asked.

Aunt Sophia pointed to the machine.

"The machine does not function the way it is intended to. It is not complete but others will not listen."

I wonder if that means Damien.

"What do you mean by dangerous?" Dorie asked. She is a worry wart as is, do not need to add to that level of anxiety.

Aunt Sophia was quiet. It looked like she was trying to decide whether to trust us with the knowledge.

"Destroy the machine." Ghost Sophia yelled.

She flew up to the top of the machine looking down on us.

"But this is extraordinary! I can't destroy it." Brad said.

Everything in the room started swirling around us. Ghost Sophia began screaming. We had to cover our ears and duck to the floor. We crawled out the door and back downstairs. The screaming didn't stop. She means business.

We left the building before she done more harm.

None of us spoke for awhile. I was thinking about the machine and wondering why it would be dangerous. If it worked one could see their future and yes in a way that's dangerous. Especially, if you change the course of events.

But I have a feeling something entirely different is meant here.

TWENTY

We sat in silence at the table in the middle of the cave town. I chomped on a sandwich and drank some Pepsi.

Dorie was the first to speak.

"We could destroy it. The plans are in the lab book if one ever wanted to rebuild."

"What I don't understand is it is basically in sight so Damian has to know it is there. What does he need with you Annie?" Brad asked.

"The rock. He doesn't know how they work together. My guess he thinks grandpa knows where the main rock is to give it enough power."

"Why didn't he go to your grandpa?"

"Grandpa never liked him."

Duh, grandpa knew his family, the mining company. Makes sense now. I thought grandpa was being over protective when I dated Damian. Another connection to research. Interesting.

"I say destroy it, so Damian doesn't by chance he finds the rocks. We can rebuild later in a private location. Put the pieces in the lab. He doesn't know it's there, right?" Dorie asked.

"As far as I know he doesn't." Brad answered.

"I hate to destroy it, but I don't want Damian to have it either. I bet Ghost Sophia will disappear once we do. Sometimes ghosts hang back because of unfinished business."

"Wish we could use it once before we destroy it." Brad said.

"I don't think ghost Sophia would allow that. Plus, the rock is missing." Dorie said.

"Any of the rocks in your store be the magic one?" asked Brad.

"No. They are too small. I'm guessing the machine needs a pretty large one."

"I don't know. The street lights are small rocks and they are putting out some bright energy."

Something to ask grandpa, he did do the mining.

It took most of the evening to dissemble the machine and haul it piece by piece to the lab. Dorie tagged it all and jotted down in the lab book what each piece was. Now the lab book needs to be hidden well in the lab. I can not keep it with the journals in case Damian gets a hold of them.

Once we were done ghost Sophia flew away. No words no thank you. Wonder if we will see her again. Brad was sad, he really likes his Aunt and misses her.

"Maybe she can rest in peace now." he said walking out of the library.

"Where do you guys want to sleep at?" I asked.

"I would love to sleep by the waterfall." Dorie said.

"But that is hard ground, there are beds in there." I pointed to the living quarters.

"I'd rather not sleep where things were flying around me." She grabbed her backpack and headed to the waterfall.

Ok, it is pretty nice and calming there. I am exhausted. It didn't take long for me to pass out.

Clank clank.

"Ouch" Brad hopping on one foot.

I jolted up.

"What are you doing?" I asked.

"Sorry. I thought I heard someone back in the tunnel, got up, hit my toe on the rock and then knocked my plate off the rock trying to catch myself."

"Ouchy. What did you hear?"

"I thought a voice. I was going to sneak up on whoever it was."

"Well, you can count that out." I laughed.

"How does Dorie sleep through all this?"

"A tornado could hit and she would sleep through it. I use to do funny things to her all the time growing up and take a picture." I laughed.

"Knew you were to not be trusted." He winked.

"Do we still go check it out?" I asked looking towards the tunnel leading to his cottage.

Brad shook his head yes. He grabbed a flashlight and walked cautiously to the tunnel. I followed as quiet as possible.

We got to the entrance and stood to the side out of the way. He quickly shone the light down. Nothing.

"I bet you scared them off with your plate falling."

"Maybe."

We walked back to where we were sleeping and Dorie was GONE!

"Maybe she had to go the bathroom." I said trying to not think the worst.

"Normally, I would say yes, but those voices. Maybe they were not in the tunnel. I was half asleep."

"Now, you are scaring me."

I searched through her things. Flashlight still there. No way would she go without that. I really think she would have screamed seeing me gone.

I ran towards the cave town. I heard Brad's footsteps behind me. Where would someone take her? Where would I take someone?" It must be Damian. There must be another way into the cave. Brad grabbed my arm and made me stop. He put his hand over my mouth and pointed to the living quarters where the machine had been, a light shone and a silhouette in the window.

"I bet Damian discovered the machine was gone and took Dorie as a bargaining tool." Brad whispered.

"But we can't give him the machine. It no longer exists. I know he is a prick but I doubt a killer." Not real sure anymore about his actions.

"Killer. Would he go that far?"

"If we have nothing to give, maybe. We got to get to her and free her."

"A distraction will bring them out. Where's ghost Sophia when you need her."

"Maybe the library?" i shrugged my shoulders.

We snuck quietly to the library.

"Psst."

I looked at him, like really. Seriously.

"I don't know how to call a ghost. Plus, we can't be loud in case one of them goes out into the table area."

"What if she is back in the lab? We didn't completely destroy the machine. She might feel she still has to watch over it."

"You are pretty smart for a girl."

I hit his arm over that comment. I reached for the secret book to open the passageway. At least in the lab we can turn the light on and talk normal. And I need to pee.

"Feel better?" Brad asked when I walked out of the lab bathroom.

"Tremendously! Will be even better when Dorie is back with us."

"I know. I feel to blame. If I had not agreed to help Damian neither one of you would be in danger."

"Then Damian would have come after me alone. I don't think that would have stopped him. This machine is valuable to the right buyer. He must be having money problems. Never thought he was one for excitement."

"Mean he was a boring boyfriend?"

"No, he was simple. Normal movie dates and lots of time on his farm. This adventure is so not him."

"Perhaps it was a cover for the real him. He could have been playing you back then."

"But he never asked anything about this place."

"He might have been observing. Where does his wife fit in? Did she go to school with you?"

"No, she was from a town twenty miles away."

"Another words, you know nothing about her. She could be in on this."

"No, she kicked him out because of last weekend."

"So he says. You still believe what he tells you."

That made me mad. Am I really that gullible.

"Enough. Miss Sophia!" I yelled.

Nothing.

"You try. She's your Aunt."

"Aunt Sophia! We need your help."

Nothing.

"What are we going to do to get Dorie?"

"Aunt Sophia, please!"

She appeared in front of Brad.

"Our friend is in trouble. We need you to scare the people who are holding her while we sneak in and free her. Please."

"Why? You didn't destroy the machine."

"It's not useable. The man who wants it will be the one you are scaring. I doubt he will come back down here. Find your scary face."

She made the most frightening, ugly face I have ever seen. If I had not went pee a few minutes ago I would have peed my pants.

"Not us!" Brad yelled.

Out she went!

We ran down the tunnel to the library. We stood by the front door watching across the street. First one to run out was Damian. Then the two goons followed. They ran towards the pond. We dashed into the living quarters. Dorie was tied up on the couch.

She looked a bit pale.

"That was the scariest ghost ever! Was that your Aunt?"

Brad shook his head yes while undoing all the ropes. We went out the door.

"We can't go the way they went." I said.

Brad got out the map. He pointed to a possible entry the opposite way.

Another tunnel behind the power building. The tunnel was longer than the first one. It was a bit scary not knowing where it may come out at. I couldn't stop looking back to see if they had turned around. So far no. She scared them good.

"A door. Hope we don't need a key." Brad said trying the door knob. It opened. Thank goodness.

"I bet they came through here and forgot to lock it. I won't forget." He locked it once we were out.

"Strange they didn't run this way." Dorie said.

"They panicked, ran the way their instincts told them."

He always has an answer. I'm wondering if I'm being too gullible with him too.

The door was near the old train depot. Makes sense if they ever sold the rocks, be the way to ship them out years ago. Another question to ask grandpa.

Dorie came to my place and decided to stay the night so we weren't alone. Brad wanted to but I said no. Dorie and I need to talk. We need to brainstorm. Sucks our exploring was ended so soon. The sun will be up in another hour. We have all Saturday to talk and sleep. Families think we are gone.

TWENTY ONE

We crashed on the couch, her on one end, me on the other, like when we were kids. I don't know what I would have done if we had not found her and rescued her. I would hope Damian wouldn't hurt her but I never thought he would kidnap someone either. Guess I don't know him.

I looked at the clock on the wall, 1:00pm. About five hours of sleep, plenty. I made us breakfast even though its lunch time. We had sandwiches last night.

"Oh, that smells heavenly." Dorie said stretching.

"Figured a full stomache would be better for brainstorming our next step."

"Definitely."

"Probably good you go back to school on Monday. I worry he will try again to kidnap you."

"I don't think he will. It fell apart and I think after seeing him run from Ms. Scary Sophia he will hide for awhile. Might be the best time to go back down there."

"Seriously, you would go again? I figured you would never again."

"Oh, heck, not going to let him scare me. Just don't leave me alone again. I think it will be fine."

"Actually, I think the place we need to go is Brad's Aunt's house. I think the place is a missing piece there."

"But the cave is so cool. And I doubt Damian will go down for awhile."

"I don't want to take a chance."

Dorie pouted.

"Please, don't do that." I said.

More pouting.

"You really saw the most interesting parts already. We need the map to see if there are other hidden tunnels, but Brad has both parts."

"Is the house big?"

"Oh, yes and there's a third floor with a locked door. Sounds mysterious to me. He thinks it's a ballroom. I think it's full of his family history, old trunks, photos, etc."

"Do we call and ask to come over or break in?" Dorie was excited. I couldn't help but laugh.

"Break in!"

We devoured our food, showered, packed a burglar's backpack and off we went to Brad's. Maybe we will get lucky and he is at the farm catching up on work. I remembered a road right before his place with lots of trees. I parked the car and we walked down his road. The car is hidden good.

If we have to escape there are lots of trees to hide around. So exciting. Love it. I've never seen Dorie this excited. College is changing my friend. In a good way, though.

"That is a gorgeous house. How did we never know it was here?" Dorie said.

"My thoughts exactly."

I didn't see Brad's car out front. We might get lucky.

"Look for a window we can get in through." I said.

Dorie walked up to the front door, and opened it.

"Why not the door?" Dorie laughed.

"Shh. He might be here."

"Sorry." she whispered.

No TV or radio on. Quiet as can be.

"If the third floor is locked, how are we getting in?"

"First, I think try the den for a key. If not I brought some tools." I said.

"Have you ever used these tools?"

"Well, no, but TV shows make it look easy."

Dorie rolled her eyes.

"Den is this way. Let's do this quickly since we don't know when he will be back. I assume late but who knows."

"What if he goes by your house?"

"Duh, we are not there and he is not my keeper."

"He can be mine." Dorie mumbled.

We looked through drawers, boxes, and even behind books. No key. Where would I hide a key?

"Open the books up! I bet it's in a book!"

"Why do you say that?"

"A hunch. Drawers are obvious. The desk is obvious. This was his Aunt's house. Where was the map, a book. I bet Aunt Sophia hid that. Do you remember what kind of book the map was in?"

"No I don't." Dorie answered.

He has almost as many books as me. This could take a while. Funny how he told me I could read any of them.

"Look for books on rocks!" He knew I was looking at those at the store, plus he said his Aunt had rocks.

Dorie opened a book and inside was a key, several.

"Oh, they cut a hole in the pages. Sad for the book." Dorie said.

"Take them all and put the book back. Awesome. So cool."

I grabbed her hand and we ran for the stairs. Time is ticking.

There are seven keys and not a single one worked. I have never been so bummed. Really, fate, you do this to me.

"Guess break out those tools." Dorie said.

Dug through the bag. Pulled out the tool.

"A paperclip, really." Dorie said.

"Well, ya. They use hair pins all the time. Paperclip same concept when unbent."

I fiddled with the lock forever. Not as easy as I thought.

Click.

We grinned at each other. I slowly opened the door. Dark as the darkest night without the moon. I felt for a switch. Found it!

"Holy moly! That is not what I think it is!" Dorie exclaimed running for the huge machine in the middle of a ballroom.

"Guess he wasn't lying. Wonder if he knows this is here?"

"that Aunt Sophia designed a second machine." Dorie clapped her hands.

"Quite the lady. Well done. No wonder she didn't mind the other being destroyed."

Dorie flipped a few switches, nothing.

"Do you think you should do that?" I asked.

"How can you not want to flip switches? It is like popping those bubbles that come out of packages."

She has a point, laughing at her.

"Remember she was crying for a rock. I doubt is works until we find it."

Dorie grabbed a couple of the purple rocks off the table next to the machine. She ran all around the machine looking for a place to put them.

"What are you doing?" I asked.

"I remember a bit of her notes. Look for a glass door."

"Ok."

"Found it." Dorie placed the rocks in it. The machine lit up! A funny noise began like a car motor. Then a wheel of light shone off to the right side.

"Whoa!" We said at the same time.

We smiled at one another. Do we dare enter. We have no idea what to expect or if we can get back. How cool would it be to go to the future. I would even go to the past to when my grandpa was mining. It is tempting. I don't care to be stuck in time though.

"It's too big of a gamble. We have no idea how it works. We could be lost forever." I said.

Then Dorie done the unthinkable, she ran into the light.

"NO!" I heard Brad yell running through the door.

I dropped to the ground. Dorie. I lost my best friend again.

www.ingramcontent.com/pod-product-compliance
Lightning Source LLC
Chambersburg PA
CBHW052102070526
44584CB00017B/2298